Sir Humphry Davy's Published Works

June Z. Fullmer

Harvard University Press

Cambridge, Massachusetts

1969

Distributed in Great Britain by Oxford University Press, London
Library of Congress Catalog Card Number 69-18029
SBN 674-80961-0
Printed in the United States of America

For Paul

Acknowledgments

Parts of my Davy studies were supported by fellowships from the Guggenheim Foundation and from the American Council of Learned Societies. The Tulane University Council on Research also provided aid.

Librarians have offered help far beyond what might reasonably be expected. John Neu of the University of Wisconsin was generous in sharing his expertise in bibliography in the history of science. K. D. C. Vernon of the Royal Institution was gracious, helpful, and considerate in answering my queries. I. Kaye of the Royal Society provided guidance to the archives of the Royal Society. But it is to Miss Betty Mailhes of the Howard-Tilton Library, Tulane University, that I am most grateful. With unfailing courtesy and good humor she arranged the logistics of the massive program of interlibrary loans upon which the construction of this bibliography depended.

Michael Curran transliterated the Russian entries, and assisted with Swedish entries. Thomas Kuhn and Everett Mendelssohn both made useful suggestions. Robert Siegfried provided a census of the manuscripts at the Royal Institution. Miss Nancy Herman, my research assistant at Ohio State, has proved untiring as she checked many of the items in this list. Sir Harold Hartley continues to offer me warm encouragement for my Davy studies, as did the late Douglas McKie and the late J. R. Partington. It is with pleasure that I offer my public thanks to them.

Finally, I thank my many friends who long ago accepted Sir Humphry Davy as a topic of conversation, and have been patient and willing listeners to my problems. Particularly I express my gratitude to Mrs. Roberta Capers, Gerald Capers, Miss L. Shannon Dubose, Joseph Ewan, Mrs. Selma Fraiberg, Louis Fraiberg, Mrs. Catherine Fogle, Richard H. Fogle, Harold N. Lee, Mrs. Virginia McConnell, Miss Prudence Myer, Miss Jane Oppenheimer, and Mrs. Aline Taylor.

My husband, Paul P. Fullmer, made no objection when Sir Humphry Davy moved into the house and stayed an unconscionably long time. There is no way properly to express my gratitude for his understanding, assistance, and encouragement.

In spite of so long a list of indebtedness, errors and omissions in what follows are my sole responsibility, and I will be very pleased to learn of them.

Contents

Sir Humphry Davy's Published Works

Introduction

When Sir Humphry Davy died in Geneva in 1829, his elaborate public funeral in that city was the first of many tributes to him. Capping a decade of eulogies, his enduring memorial, *The collected works of Sir Humphry Davy*, appeared in 1839–1840. These nine volumes, edited by his brother, Dr. John Davy, are so impressive that they have always been taken as the definitive statement of Sir Humphry's achievement. Close examination of the literature shows, however, that the volumes are not complete. Though they do reflect the wide range of subjects which Davy investigated and do reprint the major papers on which his fame depends, omissions present a hidden obstacle to full evaluation of his accomplishments.

Attempts to list Davy's papers have been sporadic and incomplete. Shortly after his death the *Quarterly Journal of Science, Literature and the Arts* (28:149–152; 1829) published the titles of his papers that had appeared in the *Philosophical Transactions* and briefly noted eight of his separate publications. The *Royal Society's catalogue of scientific papers, 1800–1900*, provides a further guide to his work, although it does not include book-length publications, and the differentiation between translations, abstracts, reviews, and reprints of original papers is not always clear. Moreover, Davy's publications which were not purely scientific are omitted. J. C. Poggendorf's *Biographische-literarisches Handwörterbuch zur Geschichte der exacten Wissenschaften* also presents a partial listing. J. R. Partington's *A history of chemistry* (1964; 4:320–373) furnishes a valuable commentary on many of Davy's publications. G. C. Boase and W. P. Courtney indicate some of Davy's publications and many publications about him in their *Bibliotheca Cornubiensis* (London: Longman, 1874, 1882, I, 106–111; III, 1150–1152). Similar material can also be found in Boase's *Collectanea Cornubiensa* (Truro: Netherton and Worth, 1890, col. 193–196).

It is the purpose of this bibliography to list the published writings of Sir Humphry Davy that appeared during his lifetime and posthumously. The list has been expanded by means of a cataloguing device to show translations of his papers and to include the reports of his experimental findings printed prior to the official versions. Critical reviews in journals not exclusively devoted to scientific subjects have also been catalogued. These derived publications, abstracts, reviews, translations, and early reports, are included here because they frequently forced Davy to further publication.

CONTEMPORARY TRANSMISSION OF DAVY'S IDEAS

Davy was for a time a leading and controversial member of the international scientific community. A web of communications bound the community together, and although national isolationism and political upheaval at times severed one or another part of it, the web was never totally disrupted. Davy's publications received all the kinds of publicity available to an early nineteenth century natural philosopher. For that reason the pattern prevailing in the list that follows is of interest not only for what it reveals of Davy, but as an exemplar of how scientific news was transmitted in this period.

Immediately Davy's papers were read to the Royal Society, reports of them were published in British scientific and more general journals, and sometimes in the newspapers. (A similar pattern prevailed for papers other than those read to the Royal Society.) Fellows of the Royal Society and other interested parties wrote letters about the work to their distant colleagues, and some of their letters were published verbatim, or in translation, in American and Continental journals. Not all of the reports were accurate; a letter was sometimes too brief to do complicated matters justice, and sometimes the reporters had misunderstood the work. Davy, when he became aware of poor reporting, sought to put it right, and, as a result, some of those early abstracts were corrected in subsequent issues of the journals. In particular, the preliminary reports of Thomas Thomson almost invariably required correction, expansion, or modification (see, for example, 1813:3A).

Davy himself contributed to the apparent unreliability of some of the reports, for occasionally he exploited the time between reading of a paper and its actual publication to modify his statements or to do further experiments (1813:4A). In one instance, his changes were so numerous that he could not, in good conscience, make silent corrections; to expand and modify his views he published a twenty-page paper as an "Appendix" to a Bakerian lecture (1809:1).

Once the official version of the paper had appeared, Davy lost no time in sending offprints to his colleagues and to journal editors. Sometimes he expanded the printed version with handwritten notes interpolated into the text in appropriate places (1809:9); at other times his letter of transmittal for the offprints contributed additional scientific information (1810:14T). In keeping with contemporary practice, some journals reprinted Davy's original text; others reviewed the printed versions. Continental editors exercised several options. Generally the Swiss editors of *Bibliothéque britannique* commissioned full-length or nearly full-length translations; as a result, there were periods when entire issues of their journal were given over to Davy's works (1800:2C). Gay-Lussac and Thenard, who controlled the Parisian *Annales de Chimie*, sometimes reprinted parts of the Swiss translations and sometimes arranged for a complete, new translation (for example, 1810:16T). At times Davy's covering letters and added notes were appended to the new translations (1814:1T); on other occasions the editors published them as separate items (1809:9T). If a paper was long (and some of Davy's papers were very long) or if the translation was to be delayed, both the Swiss and French editors might first publish extracts from it. It was not unusual for the French to publish essays which claimed to extract the essence of the Swiss translations. These abstracts, however, are often such in name only, in spite of titles proclaiming them as written by Davy, for what was published was frequently a highly colored and prejudicial commentary on the original paper (1809:1C). A third French version of many of Davy's papers appeared in *Journal de physique*. The aged republican and phlogistonist J. C. Dela-Métherie, who edited the journal, translated many of Davy's papers (for example, 1810:14T), or made long extracts from them, guided by his sometimes eccentric personal opinions. He further summarized in his annual reports what for him represented Davy's main scientific contributions. These retrospective essays guaranteed that Davy's findings were reviewed and re-reviewed, sometimes for three or four consecutive years.

German members of the international scientific community eventually had access to the most accurate renderings of Davy's works. When the Napoleonic disturbances were at their peak, the

Germans had to depend for their scientific news on what the French allowed to cross the borders. Long delays in transmission of original papers between England and France were not unusual; it took longer for them to arrive in Germany. Many months had elapsed after English publication of some of Davy's papers before Gehlen, Gilbert, and Schweigger, the chief German editors, received the French and Swiss translations and reports. Sometimes German versions of Davy's papers had to be made by collating the available French versions (for example, 1806:3c). When Davy finally realized how long the Germans had had to wait, and how interested they were in his work, he began to send them offprints directly, usually via diplomatic pouch, routed through Sweden. Such roundabout transmission could still be frustrated by political difficulties and the uncertainties of weather and travel. As a general rule, after 1815 the Germans had access to the English texts. German editors, well aware of the substantive differences between the reports and the translations into French that came to them, congratulated themselves in print on the superior accuracy of German publication.

Passage of the texts of Davy's papers through so many hands, and, in particular, through the hands of Davy's scientific and political enemies, meant that some of his very revolutionary ideas could be garbled, misrepresented, or even emended. Prieur and De la Rive, two of the Continental commentators, freely interjected their own ideas into Davy's papers, and both covertly and overtly displayed their bias for scientific points of view other than what they were ostensibly reporting. Occasionally, too, their efforts were marred by carelessness. Almost every presentation in the French journals of numerical data from Davy's papers is suspect. Decimals strayed to the left and to the right or vanished completely; unfortunately, from the context it is not always obvious that errors have been perpetrated. Whole sentences in some of the translations make no sense, or are just wrong. In many of the Continental versions, the very large number of slight misrepresentations accumulate an impression of Davy's scientific insights that is at once faulty and inadequate. Some translations omitted paragraphs, or entire sections, without indicating deletions. At times the French presentations removed from Davy's prose both grace and graciousness. Editors emended the texts to clarify what translators found obscure. Footnotes were transported into the body of the paper or, sometimes, ignored; new notes were added. De la Rive on occasion signed his own additions "D.", and unless the French text is compared with the original there is no way of determining whether the "D." stands for Davy or De la Rive (1810:16c). As a result, for a determination of what Davy's work meant to the Continental scientific community it is necessary to study these derived versions along with his original papers.

The saga of communication does not end here, for eventually Davy saw some of the prior reports, the abstracts, and the translations. His letters show that he regarded the situation as calamitous and that he tried valiantly to guarantee that what his colleagues at home and abroad read under his name was a just reproduction or interpretation. When he was sufficiently grieved by these derived publications he sent corrections directly to the foreign editors (for example, 1808:3T). Often the corrections got published several months after the publication they were to put right (1808:3T). As a result, consecutive reading of the journals today generates a faulty impression. Editors, authors, abstractors, and translators made no attempt to conceal the supposed shortcomings of their rivals, or of Davy; their carping in footnotes and in appended comments was sometimes subtle and sometimes blatant. On the other hand, they praised their own reliability and their speed in getting information to a waiting scientific community. Davy's protests could be interpreted by some as the cry of a man especially hypersentitive, shrill, and waspish, or, even worse, of a man who did not know his own scientific mind. Davy, for his part, was equally quick to judge; he reacted strongly whenever he thought he had been unfairly represented. Like his contemporaries he saw his own work as part of his nation's bid for eminence. Releasing controversial scientific opinions and findings to a world politically unsettled and plagued by slow communications encouraged partisanship and hot-tempered criticism. Yet in spite of the barriers to complete understanding of his work, Davy's international scientific influence was for a time very great.

DAVY'S PUBLISHED WORK

BOOKS. Davy's first published book was *Researches, chemical and philosophical; chiefly concerning nitrous oxide* (1800:2); his last was the posthumously published *Consolations in travel* (1830:1). In the intervening years he published five others, of which two were collections of shorter papers. All of his books were translated into at least one other language, and most of them went through several editions and reprintings. *The elements of agricultural chemistry* (1813:6) based on the lectures Davy gave to the Board of Agriculture beginning in 1803, easily his most widely studied work, went through many editions and reprintings in his lifetime and after. I have located citations of translations in French, Spanish, German, Italian, and Russian. No attempt has been made in this list to hazard into the complexities of publishing in the early nineteenth century, but some of the problems announce themselves in the many entries for this title.

Davy's *Elements of chemical philosophy* (1812:6) was his sole chemical text. Although the title bears the legend "Part I, Volume I," only this portion was published or, indeed, written. His *Salmonia* (1828:4), which exists in two editions, was first published as the work of "An Angler," but the anonymity was transparent, and the book was known to have been by Davy from the very start. His collected papers on the safety lamp went through several editions (1816:12). His *Discourses to the Royal Society* (1827:1) the least well known of his book-length works, contains not only the St. Andrew's Day lectures he delivered during his tenure as President of the Royal Society, but his inaugural discourse as well. Each of his books received critical attention in scientific journals at home and on the Continent, and in journals, like the *Edinburgh Review*, with an even wider reading audience.

ROYAL SOCIETY PAPERS. Davy's most important scientific work is reported in the forty-six papers he presented to the Royal Society. In the first (1801:2), read on 18 June 1801, Davy showed how a Voltaic battery could be constructed from a single metallic species. His last paper (1828:2), read 20 November 1828, discussed the electrical properties of the torpedo, regarded as the prime example of an "animal battery." During his career he read six Bakerian lectures, the first of which, on the relations between chemical reactions and electricity, was awarded Napoleon's minor prize in electrochemistry (1806:3). His subsequent Bakerians announced the isolation of sodium, potassium, barium, strontium, calcium, and magnesium, and demonstrated the existence of fluorine, aluminum, and boron. His 1810 Bakerian lecture (1810:16) continued his demonstration of the elemental nature of chlorine. His final Bakerian lecture (1826:1), read 8 June 1826, returned to the subject of his first, and continued his discussion of the relations between chemical reactivity and electricity.

Nicholson's *Journal*, the *Philosophical Magazine*, and *Annals of Philosophy* reprinted all of Davy's papers from *Philosophical Transactions*, with one exception. On 9 November 1815 his first paper on the miner's safety lamp was read to the Royal Society (1815:6). So important did the Council of the Royal Society judge it to be that they authorized its first printing in *Philosophical Magazine*; its subsequent appearance in *Philosophical Transactions* was a reprinting.

PAPERS IN SCIENTIFIC AND TECHNICAL JOURNALS. Davy published many of his papers in scientific journals other than the *Philosophical Transactions*. His earliest scientific papers appeared in *Contributions to physical and medical knowledge* (1799:6 and 7), edited by Thomas Beddoes, and in Nicholson's *Journal* (for example, 1799:8 and 9). After he had moved from Bristol to the Royal Institution in London, he and Thomas Young together edited and wrote much of the *Journal of the Royal Institution*.[1] Here Davy contributed original papers (for example, 1802:8), a paper with Thomas Wedgwood as co-author (1802:9), and many abstracts of papers by others that had appeared in Continental journals (for example, 1802:6). In the list that follows the citations for these abstracts include those for the papers Davy abstracted; when Davy added critical comments, they have been noted (1802:10).

The *Journal of the Royal Institution* was reactivated in 1816 as the *Journal of the Sciences and the Arts*, with William Thomas Brande as editor. (The first *Journal* ceased in 1803, after eighty pages of volume 2 had appeared. Apparently, the only complete copy of this *Journal* in the United States is that in the Linda Hall library.) Davy gave Brande several papers, including some of those on the miner's lamp (1816:3). Brande was eager to publish works that would attract a wide readership—Davy's fame made that automatic—but he angered Davy greatly by a premature, unauthorized publication of Davy's private report to Sir Joseph Banks about the unrolling of the Herculaneum papyri (1819:1). Later Davy was to write of Brande's "journal jobs," although his boycott of the journal was not at that time apparent. Davy helped to launch other new journals; both the *Annals of Philosophy* and the

---

[1] J. Z. Fullmer, *Chymia* 9 (1964): 97–116.

Transactions of the Royal Geological Society of Cornwall contain contributions by him in their first and in some subsequent volumes.

On several occasions Davy contributed papers directly to Continental journals. In DelaMétherie's *Journal de physique* he published three papers in French, partly because he despaired of getting good translations in the Parisian journals, and partly because of his continuing controversy with the French. Originally he had hoped to publish them in *Annales de chimie*, but Gay-Lussac and Thenard denied his request. DelaMétherie published the papers, after Davy appealed to him, but by so doing DelaMétherie jeopardized his relations with leading French scientists and his own security as well (1810:11, 12, 13). Davy read his paper on the nature of the deposits formed at the baths at Lucca (1821:1) to the Royal Academy of Naples, and it was published first in translation in their journal. He did not himself describe his experiments made at Vesuvius on erupted lavas, but the Prince of Denmark, who had accompanied him on the excursion and assisted him in the operation, provided the published description in the same journal (1820:1).

LETTERS. Many of Davy's letters found their way into print. Some of his papers to the Royal Society were, as was customary, in letter format (for example, 1812:5). His paper to the Cornish Royal Geological Society (1818:3) was addressed to Henry Boase, the secretary of the new society. Likewise, his earliest reports on the feasibility of inhaling nitrous oxide and on electrochemical researches were published as extracts from letters he addressed to William Nicholson (for example, 1799:8). In addition, he sent to several journals brief letters that reported new findings or revised his opinions of older ones (for example, 1806:1).

For a while Davy performed analyses requested by various members of the Royal Institution and by the Board of Agriculture, and authorized by the Board of the Royal Institution. A few of his reports of such analyses, drafted as letters, appeared either as appendices to larger reports, or embedded in them. His analysis of a lead ore from Sir John Sinclair's estate in Caithness (1804:5) and his analysis of the fresh lake waters in the Scilly Isles are examples (1808:5) of this kind of publication. Very early in Davy's career Thomas Beddoes published the letters in which Davy reported his analysis of commercial nitrous (that is, nitric) acid, and his testimony about certain treatments administered at the Pneumatic Institution (1800:8).

As President of the Royal Society from 1820 to 1825, and during his terms as secretary from 1807 on, Davy was involved in much of the society's official correspondence. Some of the letters he wrote expressing the opinions of the Council were printed, usually in papers by others. Letters to John Herapath and John Frederick Daniell (1821:2 and 1825:2) are examples.

To his sorrow, Davy's papers and lectures were repeatedly reported by the newspapers. From his private correspondence it would appear that he often despaired of insuring accuracy in those reports. As far as I can discover, he published only one letter of protest, that to the editor of *The Times* on 17 October 1824 (1824:5). Here he defended the scientific merits of his ship-protection scheme and his personal integrity as well.

In the list that follows, letters have not been included that were subsequently published in biographical treatments.

LECTURES. Davy went to the Royal Institution in 1800. Until he resigned in 1812, he lectured in every season. Publication of these lectures was haphazard.[2] Few verbatim transcripts have been preserved, but the popular and the scientific press abstracted many of them. In the bibliography that follows, abstracts have been cited, even though the full text did not appear. One of his lecture series on geology was abstracted and published by Thomas Allan (1811:7). (Michael Faraday's famous digest of a Davy lecture series of which he made a fair bound copy, in order to present it to Davy as a token of his interest in natural philosophy, is preserved in the Royal Institution.) John Davy located and published the complete texts of some lectures, and excerpts from others. These have been included, set off by braces, { }, if they are not available elsewhere. (For other lectures, see "Manuscripts" below.) One of his lectures on the reorganization of the Royal Institution was republished as recently as 1916 (1810:2R). Davy wrote syllabi to guide his audience at the Royal Institution and at the Board of Agriculture (1802:1; 1803:1). The latter syllabus is a scarce Davy item. Only one copy, that in the collection of the late John Fulton of Yale, has come to light. Doubtless other copies exist, for John Paris, Davy's early and "official" biographer, had access to one.

---

[2] His lecturing procedure was evidently much like that he recommended to John Dalton (W. C. Henry, *Memoirs of the life and scientific researches of John Dalton*, London, 1854, pp. 49–50). For any series, he wrote only the first lecture in detail; he drafted carefully only a paragraph or two of the subsequent lectures.

ABSTRACTS. As already mentioned, when Davy edited the *Journal of the Royal Institution* he published in it many abstracts of Continental papers. He also reported on some papers read to the Royal Society, by Chenevix, Roebuck, and others (for example, 1802:44, 45) and wrote abstracts of some of his own publications. These have been included along with the citation for the papers he abstracted.

PARLIAMENTARY PAPERS. Davy testified from time to time before parliamentary committees, either as the official representative of the Royal Society, or as Professor of the Royal Institution. Searching parliamentary reports for the early nineteenth century is difficult, but I have discovered a few instances in which Davy either testified verbally to a committee or submitted a written report to them. His remarks on the efficiency of gas lighting is an example of his oral testimony (1823:6); his letter on the breeding of salmon (1824:2), printed as an appendix in the Report of the Select Committee on Salmon Fisheries, is an example of a written report.

POEMS. Davy's first publications were poems (1799:1, 2, 3, 4, and 5), and he continued to write poetry for the rest of his life.[3] One of his poems, "Lines written on recovering from a serious illness," was said by his brother to have been published as a broadside, but a specimen has not yet been found. In 1807 he was rumored to be preparing a complete book of his poems, but it does not appear that he actually did so. Thus, though he had some reputation as a poet it seems to be based on manuscript verses circulated among his friends and acquaintances. Davy did, however, write the prologue to "The Honey-Moon," a play by John Tobin. The text of the Prologue, which he wrote a few hours before opening night, in collaboration with a friend named Sotheby, was spoken on that occasion and has been included in several copies of the play (1805:1).

MISCELLANEOUS WRITINGS. In addition to poetry Davy produced some literary essays: three that he wrote under pseudonyms for *The Director*, a journal edited by Thomas Dibdin, are here included (1807:3, 4, 5; the last entry cites the evidence for claiming Davy as the author of them). The section "Vegetables" in Abraham Rees's *Cyclopedia* (1817:6) was also his. Other sections in that very

[3] J. Z. Fullmer, *Chymia* 6 (1960):102–126.

large work may likewise have been by him, but no evidence has appeared on which to base attribution. Davy was also the chief author (with Sir Thomas Stamford Raffles) of the first prospectus for the proposed London Zoological Society (1825:1); the second prospectus was apparently the work of Raffles alone.[4]

One entry in this list possibly not by Davy is a review of, and essay about, Aldini's electrical experiments (1803:13). That Davy was indeed familiar with and interested in Aldini's work can be seen from his abstract of Aldini's paper to the Royal Society (1802:48), but more evidence than what has been noted will be necessary for definite attribution of authorship.

MANUSCRIPT COLLECTIONS

In spite of the vicissitudes of more than a century and in spite of Davy's careless treatment of his manuscripts, a large quantity of this kind of material has been preserved. There are Davy items in libraries and collections all over the world, but the three largest caches are in the archives of the Royal Society, the Royal Institution, and the Royal Geological Society of Cornwall at Penzance. Since this list deals only with published works, no entries have been made for manuscripts, with the exception of the forty manuscripts in the Royal Society library from which the printer set Davy's papers for *Philosophical Transactions*. Usually Davy had the fair copy of his papers made by an amanuensis (in some instances, after 1812, Michael Faraday acted in this capacity), but he marked the papers himself for the printer and also made last minute corrections and changes. Where these manuscripts exist a note has been inserted in the bibliography after the citation for the first published version of the paper; each entry includes the Royal Society catalog number for the item.

The Davy collection at the Royal Institution is greater than that at the Royal Society, more personal, and markedly more chaotic. At first it was assumed that this horde could be used to establish a precise canon for the published works, but study of it showed that the bibliography has to be one of the keys to ordering the Royal Institution collection. Two authors have indicated some of the problems the user of the Davy materials may encounter. Colin A. Russell examined the collection from the point of view of

---

[4] Lady Sophia Raffles, *Memoir of the life and public services of Sir Thomas Stamford Raffles* (London, 1830), pp. 588–591.

trying to determine the genesis of Day's electrochemical theories.[5] K. D. C. Vernon, in his valedictory talk to the Library Circle of the Royal Institution,[6] provided a census of the Davy manuscripts, along with recommendations for their preservation.

Part of the Royal Institution's collection reflects the care and devotion of Michael Faraday, for while Davy had little interest in the preservation of his notebooks, Faraday did, and he assembled some of them. At least one notebook came to the Royal Institution as a result of its chance discovery in an Oxford book shop by John Fulton. That part of the Royal Institution collection devoted to Davy letters owes its bulk to gifts made in 1925 by Sir Humphry Davy Rolleston.

Most celebrated of all the items are the four folio "Laboratory Notebooks" for the periods 1805–1809, 1809–1812, 1813–1821, and 1821–1829. (Housed with them is a fifth notebook covering the period 1830–1859 with entries by Faraday and William Thomas Brande.) It is here that one can find the account of the discovery of potassium (a "captl. expt. proving the decompn of *Potash*") and Davy's admonitions to his young laboratory assistants on laboratory cleanliness. ("*Objects much wanted* in the Laboratory of the Royal *Institution*; Cleanliness, Neatness & Regularity.— ... There must be in the Laboratory *Pen, Ink & paper & wafers* and these must not be kept in the Slovenly manner in which they usually are Kept. I am now writing with a pen & ink such as was never used in any other place.—") Since these note books were the "public laboratory record" (the term is John Davy's) almost all of the entries are dated and their chronology is orderly; as a result they are often quoted. Faraday is responsible for their preservation. In 1829 he wrote in the front of the first volume: "These two volumes contain the Experimental notes made in the Laboratory of the Royal Institution from October 1805 to October 1812 during which time *Sir H. Davy* was Professor of Chemistry. After I knew Sir H. Davy he occasionally tore away leaves upon which notes had been written that he might carry the data home for consideration but I presume that during the time he resided in the house of the Institution there would be no induce-ment to do so and that these two volumes have been but little injured in that way. For their future security I have this day paged the leaves regularly. There are 265 pages in this volume and 691

5 *Ann. Sci.* 19 (1963): 255–271.
6 *Proc. Roy. Inst.* 31 (1966): 241–258.

in the other not one of which is wanting." The notebooks are in fairly good condition but alterations that come with age are beginning to take their toll. Vernon suggested that they be reproduced in microform or be made available to scholars in Xerox copy. Unfortunately this has not yet been done.

These laboratory notebooks contain no item prior to 1805. This deficiency is partially corrected by "Personal Notebooks," forty-two in all, which span the period 1795–1829. In this collection there is one called "Physical Journal" which contains items from November 1800 and a description of four weeks of experiments at the Royal Institution from 11 March 1801. Extensive as the collection is, it has not been exhaustively exploited for more than a century. To be sure, large portions of it were transcribed by John Davy in his biographies of Sir Humphry; and Bence-Jones, Thorpe, Treneer, and Hartley have all used extracts from the "Personal Notebooks" (see below, Biographies, for specific references). Yet much remains to be mined. Reasons for such apparent neglect are not hard to discover. Parts of the notebooks written in pencil on adjacent pages have already blurred or rubbed nearly to extinction. Some notebooks have had laboratory chemicals spilled on them, and pages so exposed are brittle, cracked, or brown; some of them have disappeared entirely.

Davy's own work habits caused other kinds of difficulties. Davy was often in a hurry. When ideas came to him he dashed them down immediately, whether he was in the laboratory, at a meeting, being jolted in a carriage, or at his leisure at home. He doodled and drew pictures over what had earlier been clearly set down. When he wrote hastily his handwriting is difficult to decipher; when he wrote while traveling it is almost impossible to read. Aside from these kinds of problems, there are also many pages disfigured by ink smears and blots. When Davy made a mistake he frequently tried to remove the error by rubbing his finger through the wet ink. He seldom bothered to wipe his hand after such an "erasure," and double page spreads preserve his smudged finger marks. Ink was, of course, manufactured on the premises. Fresh, it must have varied from deepest black to pale gray. Now the color modulates from dark brown to pale tan to invisible. Pens were likewise handmade. Depending on the art of the nib-cutter and the care he took, the pen could produce fluent, legible strokes or scratches of a peculiar and sometimes indecipherable kind. Davy used any pen available.

These are only occasional frustrations. A more constant problem is that of organization. In his haste to write Davy usually did not date his entries, nor did he keep any particular notebook for any particular subject. It rarely occurred to him that a notebook had a back and a front, a top and a bottom. When he traveled he stuffed into his carriage as many notebooks as he could stow; when the urge to write seized him, he took any notebook that came to hand. As a result there is almost no continuity. The notebooks are written from back to front, upside down, and from the bottom to the top of the page. Occasionally a notebook begins with passages transcribed in the fastidious hand of Faraday, who tried to impose an order on things, but Davy's habits were so ingrained that his usual practices reassert themselves within a page or two.

These notebooks have also suffered physical alteration, by excision, by overwriting, and by blacking out. From time to time John Davy added notes to the manuscripts as a guide to what he found, and it has been assumed that any other changes are his work, too, perhaps the result of misprision. Some obliterations and excisions may represent an attempt to remove hints to Davy's private affairs. It may also be that some of the pages were removed to present to an individual desiring a "specimen," for one or two pages from this collection have found their way into manuscript collections in libraries far removed from the Royal Institution.

The third part of the Royal Institution Davy archives is classed under the rubric "Papers and Lectures." Again it is to Faraday's vigilance that we owe the preservation of the papers. A "Commonplace Book" from about 1815 contains this note written in July 1832: "It was part of my duty to copy these papers after he (Davy) had written them roughly. Sir H. Davy frequently wrote over these and then I had to copy again until a fair paper was produced which went to the Society or the printer. The originals used to be torn up or destroyed until I begged I might be allowed to keep them for myself and here they are." Faraday's description certainly accounts for part of the collection at the Royal Society and may explain why some of the earlier items are missing from that at the Royal Institution. K. D. C. Vernon has reproduced one of the double page spreads showing how Faraday created order in Davy's presentations.

The lectures that have been spared are likewise incomplete. Robert Siegfried reports that there are seventy-four of them, covering the period 1805 to 1812, and classified as follows: forty-one in chemistry, sixteen in geology, twelve in agricultural chemistry, and five in history of natural sciences. The geology lectures should be supplemented with those preserved at the Royal Geological Society of Cornwall, as Vernon has proposed. Unpublished material is included in the entire array; from it and from the abstracts and excerpts cited in the bibliography that follows many of the lecture series perhaps can be reconstructed.

Miscellaneous materials at the Royal Institution include Davy's copy of the first edition of *Salmonia* (1828:4) interleaved with notes for the second edition (1829:1), and two copies of *Elements of chemical philosophy* (1812:6) with marginal notes and interleavings (some in Faraday's hand) for a nonexistent revision or second volume. The Minute Books of the Royal Institution for the years of Davy's connection with it (the last twenty-nine years of his life), though regrettably brief, provide valuable clues about Davy's activities on committees and show, too, how he helped to formulate institution policies (see also, for example, 1810:2).

Finally, the Royal Institution has a collection of 330 Davy letters. Most of these, presented by the Rolleston family, deal with family matters, although some of them are on scientific subjects. Many of them have been published, either in part or in entirety. At present I am editing all of these letters for publication, together with more than 500 others found in various collections all over the world. The edited letters and all of the material described here, plus much else, will form the basis of my biography of Davy, already under way.

ARRANGEMENT OF THE BIBLIOGRAPHY

In the bibliography that follows, Davy's works are ordered by year of publication, and numbered consecutively within the year. If the work has been reproduced in *The Collected Works*, an asterisk follows the number. A paper read to a learned society or a public lecture that could be precisely dated is listed according to that date, rather than according to the date of its final publication. Periodical articles are arranged according to the month of publication, to the extent that that could be ascertained. References give an abbreviated title of the journal (keyed as described in the list of abbreviations below), the volume number, the year, if different from that under which it is listed, and the inclusive pages where the paper may be found. Books and other separate publications (not offprints) are listed under the year in which they were published, and placed at the end of the section, unless other information permitted more precise dating. Subsequent editions are listed under the first, along with translations, abstracts, and reviews.

Parliamentary papers are cited either according to the date of the committee session if Davy testified orally, or according to the date of his written report.

Some journals reprinted papers in their entirety from the original source. Such reprintings in journals printed in Great Britain have been cited under the letter R. Abstracts of papers or reports of work in British journals prior to their first publication are cited under the letter A. Articles of criticism or review have also been listed in the A section, and the critic's name has been noted where it was discoverable. Complete translations of Davy's original articles or books in Continental journals are cited under the heading T. Where possible the translator and the source of the text from which the translation was made are mentioned; where notes have been added they are indicated and the author of them, if known, identified. When Davy's requested changes were made in translations, these have also been cited in the T section for the paper to which they apply, even though the corrections may have appeared in a much later section of the journal. Citations for all preliminary reports or abstracts of Davy's works in the Continental journals are listed under C; where known, the source of the report and the name of the commentator have been included. In some instances in the A and C sections a fine line had to be drawn between what was an actual report, made for the sake of a report, and what was a digest, made only for the sake of attack in the balance of the paper. Whenever the latter situation prevailed, the report has been omitted from the listing.

Square brackets, [ ], distinguish interpolated items. Items in braces, { }, are publications available only in *The Collected Works*.

Major Biographies of Sir Humphry Davy

Since most of the later book-length biographies of Davy are derived chiefly from the first four, the titles have been arranged chronologically. See J. Z. Fullmer, *Science 155* (1967):285–291, for a discussion and evaluation of the works listed.

Paris, John Ayrton, *The life of Sir Humphry Davy, Bart., LL. D., late President of the Royal Society*. London: Colburn and Bentley, 1831. The work was issued both in two-volume and one-volume editions.

Davy, John, *Memoirs of the life of Sir Humphry Davy, Bart., LL. D., F.R.S.* London: Longman, Rees, Orme, Browne, Green and Longman, 1836. 2 volumes.

Davy, John, *The collected works of Sir Humphry Davy*. London: Smith and Elder, 1839. Vol. I.

Davy, John, *Fragmentary remains, literary and scientific, of Sir H. Davy with a sketch of his life and selections from his correspondence*. London: Churchill 1858.

Mayhew, Henry, *The wonders of science: or young Humphry Davy*. London: Bogue, 1855.

Thorpe, Thomas E., *Humphry Davy, poet and philosopher*. London: Cassell, 1896.

Ostwald, Wilhelm, *Psychographische Studien I. Humphry Davy*. Leipzig: Viet, 1907.

Gregory, J. C., *The scientific achievements of Sir Humphry Davy*. London: Oxford University Press, 1930.

Mogilevskii, B., *Gemfri Devi*. Moscow, 1937.

Prandtl, Wilhelm, *Humphry Davy: Jöns Jacob Berzelius*. Stuttgart: Wissenschaftliches Verlagsgesellschaft, 1948.

Kendall, James P., *Humphry Davy: 'Pilot' of Penzance*. London: Faber, 1954.

Treneer, Anne, *The mercurial chemist, a life of Sir Humphry Davy*. London: Methuen, 1963.

Hartley, Sir Harold, *Humphry Davy*. London: Nelson, 1966.

Journals for the history of science and technical journals have carried many articles which explore the facets of his life and work. The centenary of his death in 1929 saw the publication of a group of them, and the articles have continued unabated. The "Critical Bibliography" in *Isis*; Section 22, "Histoire des sciences et des techniques" of *Bulletin signalétique*; and *Chemical Abstracts* all provide guides to this growing collection of papers.

Abbreviations Used in Citations

AB	R. R. Shaw and R. H. Shoemaker, *American Bibliography.* New York, 1958. Series 4, vols. 1–21; series 5, vols. 1–3
Allgem. J. Chem.	*Allgemeines Journal der Chemie.* Leipzig. Vols. 1–10: 1798–1803
Ann. chim.	*Annales de chimie, ou recueil de mémoires concernant la chimie et les arts qui en dépendent* . . . . Paris. Vols. 1–96:1789–1815. *Annales de chimie et de physique.* Vols. 1–75: 1816–1840
Ann. chim. storia naturale	*Annale di chimica e storia naturale.* Pavia. Vols. 1–21: 1790–1802
Ann. Phil.	*Annals of Philosophy, or magazine of chemistry, mineralogy, mechanics, natural history, agriculture and the arts.* London. Vols. 1–16: 1813–1820; series 2, vols. 1–12 (also as 17–28): 1821–1826
Ann. Physik Chem.	*Annalen der Physik und Chemie.* Berlin. Vols. 1–30: 1824–1833
Ann. Physik (Halle)	*Annalen der Physik.* Halle. Vols. 1–60: 1799–1819. *Annalen der Physik und der physikalischen Chemie.* Vols. 61–76: 1819–1824
Arch. theoretische Chem.	*Archiv für die theoretische Chemie.* Jena and Berlin. Vol. 1: 1800–1802
Atti R. Accad. Napoli	*Atti della Reale Accademia delle Scienze e belle Lettere di Napoli; sezione della società reale borbonica.* Naples. Vols. 1–6: 1819–1851
Bence-Jones	Henry Bence-Jones, *The Royal Institution.* London, 1871
Bibl. brit.	*Bibliothèque britannique, ou recueil extrait des ouvrages anglais périodiques et autres* . . . . Geneva. Vols. 1–60: 1796–1815
Bibl. univ.	*Bibliothèque universelle des sciences, belles-lettres et arts* . . . *Partie des sciences.*

Geneva. Vols. 1–60: 1816–1835

BM   British Museum

BN   Bibliothèque Nationale

Bolton   Henry C. Bolton, *A select bibliography of chemistry, 1492–1892*. Washington: Smithsonian Institution, 1893. *First Supplement*, vol. 39 (Smithsonian publications no. 1170), 1899. *Second Supplement*, vol. 44, 1904

Bull. sci. soc. philomathique   *Bulletin des sciences*. Société philomathique. Paris. Vols. 1–3: 1791–1811. *Noveau bulletin*. Vols. 1–3: 1807–1812 (1808–1813). *Bulletin*. Vols. 1–11: 1814–1824

Director   *The Director: A literary and scientific journal*. London. Vols. 1–2: 1807

ECB   *The English Catalogue of Books*. London: Simpson, Low and Marston. Vols. I–VI

Edin. Phil. J.   *The Edinburgh Philosophical Journal* .... Edinburgh. Vols. 1–14: 1819–1826

Edin. Rev.   *The Edinburgh Review, or Critical Journal*. Edinburgh and London. Vols. 1–250: 1802–1929

Edinburgh   *Catalogue of the Printed Books in Edinburgh University Library*. Edinburgh: University Press. 1918. 3 vols.

Española   *Catalogo general de la Librería Española e Hispanoamericana. Años 1901 y 1930*. Vol. 2. Madrid and Barcelona: Cámaras Oficiales del Libro, 1933

Fragments   John Davy, *Fragmentary remains, literary and scientific, of Sir H. Davy ... with a sketch of his life and selections from his correspondence*. London: Churchill, 1858

Giorn. arcad.   *Giornale Arcadico di Scienze*. Rome. Vols. 1–145: 1819–1856

Giorn. fis. chim. storia nat.   *Giornale di fisica, chimica e storia naturale*. Pavia. Vols. 1–5: 1808–1817. *Giornale di fisica, chimica, storia naturale, medicina ed arti*. Vols. 1–10: 1818–1827

Heinsius   Wilhelm Heinsius, *Allgemeines Bücher-Lexicon* .... Leipzig: Gleditsch, 1817. 19 vols. in 28

HSA   *Hispanic Society of America, Catalogue of the Library*. Boston: Hall, 1962. 10 vols.

J. Chem. Physik Mineral.	*Journal für die Chemie, Physik und Mineralogie.* Berlin. Vols. 1–9: 1806–1810
J. chim. phys.	*Journal de chimie et de physique.* Brussels. Vols. 1–6: 1801–1804.
J. mines	*Journal des mines; publié par l'agence (le conseil) des mines de la république.* Paris. Vols. 1–10: 1795–1801. *Journal des mines, ou recueil de mémoires sur l'exploitation des mines* . . . . Vols. 11–38: 1802–1815
J. Nat. Phil. Chem. Arts.	*Journal of Natural Philosophy, Chemistry and the Arts.* London. Vols. 1–5: 1797–1801. Vols. 1–36: 1802–1813. (Nicholson's *Journal*)
J. phys. chim. histoire nat. arts.	*Journal de physique, de chimie, d'histoire naturelle et des arts.* Paris. Vols. 1–96: 1794–1823
J. Royal Inst.	*Journal of the Royal Institution of Great Britain.* London. Vols. 1–2: 1802–1803
Jahrb. Chem. Physik.	*Neues Journal für Chemie und Physik.* Nürnberg. Vols. 1–30: 1811–1820. *Jahrbuch der Chemie und Physik.* Vols. 31–42: 1821–1824. *Jahrbuch der Chemie und Physik, als eine Zeitschrift des Wissenschaftlichen Vereins zur Naturkenntnis und höheren Wahrheit.* Vols. 1–6 (43–54): 1825–1828. Vols. 1–3 (55–60): 1829
Kayser	Christian G. Kayser, *Vollständiges Bücher-Lexikon.* Leipzig: [Publisher varies]. 1834–1920. 42 vols. in 29
LC	Library of Congress
Life	John Ayrton Paris, *The life of Sir Humphry Davy, Bart., L.L.D., late President of the Royal Society.* London: Colburn and Bentley, 1831, 2 vols.
Lit. Gaz.	*Literary Gazette* . . . . London. 1817–1862
London Med. Rev.	*London Medical Review and Magazine* London. Vols. 1–8: 1799–1802
Mag. encyclopédique	*Magasin encyclopédique; ou journal des sciences, des lettres et des arts.* Paris. New Series, vols. 1–122: 1795–1816
Mag. naturvidensk.	*Magazin for naturvidenskaberne.* Vols. 1–10: 1825–1831
Memoirs	John Davy, *Memoirs of the life of Sir Humphry Davy, Bart., L.L.D., F.R.S.* London: Longmans, 1836. 2 vols.

Mirror	Mirror Monthly Magazine. London. Vols. 1–38: 1822–1841
Monthly Mag.	Monthly Magazine and British Register. London. Vols. 1–60: 1796–1826. Monthly Magazine; or British Register of literature, art, science . . . . Vols. 1–19: 1826–1835
Monthly Repository	Monthly Repository of Theology and General Literature. London. Vols. 1–21: 1806–1826. New series, vols. 1–5: 1827–1831
Monthly Rev.	The Monthly Review; or Literary Journal (various subtitles). London. Series 2, vols. 1–108: 1790–1825. Series 3, vols. 1–15: 1826–1830
Neues allgem. J. Chem.	Neues allgemeines Journal der Chemie. Leipzig. Vols. 1–10: 1803–1806
Neues J. Pharm. Aerzte Apoth. Chem.	Neues Journal der Pharmacie für Aerzte, Apotheker und Chemiker. Leipzig. Vols. 1-26: 1817–1833
Nicholson's Journal	See J. Nat. Phil. Chem. Arts
Parl. pap.	Great Britain. Parliamentary Papers (House of Commons series)
Phil. Mag.	Philosophical Magazine . . . . London. Vols. 1–42: 1798–1813. The Philosophical Magazine and Journal. Vols. 43–68: 1814–1826. Philosophical Magazine or Annals of Chemistry . . . . Vols. 1–11: 1827–1832
Phil. Trans.	Philosophical Transactions of the Royal Society. London.
Proc. Roy. Inst.	Notices of the Proceedings at the Meetings of the Royal Institution, with Abstracts of the Discourses Delivered at the Evening Meetings. London. From vol. 1: 1851
Quart. J. Sci.	Journal of Science and the Arts; ed. at the Royal Institution. London. Vols. 1–6: 1816–1819. Quarterly Journal of Science, Literature, and the Arts. Vols. 7–22: 1819–1827 (that is, December 1826; vol. 7 has title, Quarterly Journal of Literature, Science, and the Arts); new series, vols. 1–7 (but without volume numbering): 1827–1830
Quart. Rev.	The Quarterly Review. London. From vol. 1: 1809
Quérard	Joseph M. Quérard, La France Litteraire, ou Dictionnaire bibliographique des

	savants . . . de la France, ainsi que des litterateurs étrangers qui ont écrit en français . . . . Paris: Didot. 1827–1864. 12 vols.
Repert. Arts Manufactures	*Repertory of Arts and Manufactures.* London. Vols. 1–16: 1794–1802; series 2, vols 1–46: 1802–1825
SB	*Svenskt Boklexikon.* Aren 1830–1865. Vol. A-L. Stockholm: Linnstrom, 1883
Trans. Roy. Geol. Soc. Cornwall	*Transactions of the Royal Geological Society of Cornwall.* Penzance. From vol. 1: 1818
Trans. Roy. Soc. Edin.	*Transactions of the Royal Society of Edinburgh.* Edinburgh. From vol. 1: 1783
Trans. Soc. Arts Manuf. Comm.	*Royal Society Instituted at London for the Encouragement of Arts, Manufactures, and Commerce. Transactions.* London. Vols. 1–55: 1783–1845
Wellesley Index	*The Wellesley Index to Victorian periodicals, 1824–1900,* W. E. Houghton, ed. Canada: University of Toronto; London: Routledge and Kegan Paul. 1966. Vol. 1
Works	*The collected works of Sir Humphry Davy,* ed. John Davy. London: Smith, Elder, 1839–1840. 9 vols.
Z. Physik Math. (Wien)	*Zeitschrift für Physik und Mathematik.* Vienna, Vols. 1–10: 1826–1832

Published Works

Symbols Used in Listings

The plan and arrangement of the list is explained on pp. 15–16. The following symbols and abbreviations are those most frequently used.

A   Abstract or review of a work published in England
c   Abstract or review of a work published outside Great Britain
ns   new series of a journal
R   Reprint of a paper
s   series of a journal
T   Translation
T'   Retranslation of a work not originally published in English
★   Distinguishes items which are reprinted in *Works*
{ }   Distinguishes items included in *Works* and not published elsewhere
[ ]   Distinguishes interpolated items

1799

1. The sons of genius

    Annual Anthology 1:93–99.
    A poem signed "D. 1795" in a collection edited by Robert
    Southey. Southey hoped to spark a literary renaissance
    in the west of England by providing an outlet for the work
    of young poets. Poems by S. T. Coleridge, Southey, Davy,
    and others associated with the Bristol literary group were
    included.

2. The song of pleasure

    Annual Anthology 1:120–125.
    A poem signed "D. 1796."

3. Ode to St. Michael's Mount, in Cornwall

    Annual Anthology 1:172–176.
    A poem signed "D. 1796." A facsimile reproduction of a
    manuscript version of the poem appears in *Magazine of
    Medicine* 2 (1897):63–65.

4. The tempest

    Annual Anthology 1:179–180.
    A poem signed "D. 1796."

5. Extract from an unfinished poem on Mount's-Bay

    Annual Anthology 1:281–286.

    1799 : 1, 2, 3, 4, and 5 were reproduced in *Life*, I, 25–39.
    Dr. J. A. Paris made changes in spelling, punctuation, and
    wording.

6.★ An essay on heat, light and the combinations of light

    *Contributions to physical and medical knowledge, principally
    from the west of England, collected by Thomas Beddoes, M.D.,*
    Bristol: Biggs and Cottle, pp. 4–147.

R. *Monthly Rev.* 30:63–65.
    Reviewed by John Ferriar.
    London Med. Rev. 1:384–397.

c. *Allgem. J. Chem.* 2:510b.

Beddoes's announcement briefly abstracted Davy's paper. Davy's suggested nomenclature is described in the same journal, 5 (1800):795–796.

T. *Ann. Physik (Halle)* 12 (1802):546–552, 566–573, 574–596.

L. W. Gilbert, the editor, pointed out discrepancies in Davy's reasoning in this long abstract, even though he knew that Davy had retracted some of his speculations. (See 1799:8 and 1800:2).

Arch. theoretische Chem. 1 (1800):94–106.

Translation of Davy's section on the immateriality of heat. [Experiment III.]

7.⋆ An essay on the generation of phosoxygen, or oxygen gas: and on the causes of the colours of organic beings

Contributions to physical and medical knowledge, principally from the west of England, collected by Thomas Beddoes, M.D., Bristol: Biggs and Cottle, pp. 151–198.

Addenda to this essay and to 1799:6 are printed on pp. 199–205. In some copies p. 199 is incorrectly numbered 179. Beddoes supplied the "Specimen of an Arrangement of Bodies according to their Principles." The folded plate facing p. 211 utilized Davy's nomenclature.

A. *London Med. Rev.* 1:458–473.

[Anon.] *The Sceptic* (1800). Retford: Printed by E. Peart, and sold by West and Hughes, no. 27 Pater-Noster-Row, London, pp. 12–56.

A copy of this scarce pamphlet exists in the Bodleian library. Davy was strongly attacked by the pamphleteer, who quoted chunky excerpts from both 1799:6 and 7. John Ferriar reviewed the pamphlet in *Monthly Rev.* 35: 217–218, and included an excerpt from Davy's paper in the review.

c. *J. chim. phys.* 1 (an X):21–40.

8.⋆ Experiments and observations on the silex composing the epidermis or external bark, and contained in other parts of certain vegetables

J. Nat. Phil. Chem. Arts 3:55–56, 56–59.

Davy's letter of transmittal (pp. 55–56) was dated 11 April 1799. Pages 56–59 include a preliminary report of his first attempt to inhale nitrous oxide, a retraction of parts of 1799:6, and a description of some of the properties of strontium and barium chloride.

т. *Bibl. brit.* 11 (an VII):264–276.
J. phys. chim. histoire nat. arts 49 (an VII):202–206.
Ann. Physik (Halle) 6 (1800):109–115.
с. *Allgem. J. Chem.* 3:75–80; 4 (1800):194–195.
J. phys. chim. histoire nat. arts 49 (an VII):156; 54 (an X): 101–102.
Bibl. brit. 11 (an VII):354–355.

9. Extract of a letter to Mr. Nicholson

J. Nat. Phil. Chem. Arts 3:93.
Davy's letter, dated 17 April 1799, established that nitrous oxide can be respired.

т. *Bibl. brit.* 11 (an VII):356–358.
Ann. Physik (Halle) 2:483.
с. *Allgem. J. Chem.* 4 (1800):547–548.

10. Extract of a letter to Mr. Nicholson

J. Nat. Phil. Chem. Arts 3:138.
Davy found silex in *equisetum hyemale*. He also abstracted L. N. Vauquelin's paper—*Ann. chim.* 29 (1798):3–26)—on the composition of fowl excrements.

1800

1. Lines descriptive of feelings produced by a visit to the place where the first nineteen years of my life were spent, on a stormy day, after an absence of thirteen months

Annual Anthology 2:293–296.
A poem signed "k," possibly an abbreviation for "kolpophilos." Davy signed a letter to his Bristol associate John King in this way in June 1801. A copy of this *Annual Anthology* annotated by S. T. Coleridge (C. B. Tinker Collection, Yale) identifies the poem as having been written by Davy. A much altered text of the poem appears in *Memoirs*, I, 110–111.

2.⋆ Researches chemical and philosophical; chiefly concerning nitrous oxide, or dephlogisticated nitrous air, and its respiration

London: printed for J. Johnson, St. Pauls' Church-Yard, by Biggs and Cottle, Bristol. (xvi) 580 pp. illus.

Davy apologized for his earlier monographs on the properties of light and especially for his insistence on the idea that heat is motion (see 1799:6 and 7) in the introduction, p. xiii. Pages 497–580 are the contributions of others, including John Tobin, William Clayfield, Robert Southey, Peter Roget, Samuel Taylor Coleridge, and Thomas Beddoes, all of whom described their experiences inhaling nitrous oxide.

A. *Monthly Mag.* 11 (1801):596–597.
Monthly Rev. 35 (1801):38–44.
Reviewed by John Ferriar.

C. *Ann. chim.* 41 (an X):305–308; 42 (an X):33–38, 276–280; 43 (an X):97–100, 324–325; 44 (an XI):43–44 (with Davy's corrections), 218–220; 45 (an XI):97–102, 169–170.

A critical review and long abstract by C. L. Berthollet, reprinted from *Bibl. brit.* 19 (an X):43–66, 141–154, 321–339; 20 (an X):27–48, 217–246, 346–376. (For Davy's rejoinder see 1802:14.)

J. phys. chim. histoire nat. arts 56 (an XI):86–87.

Ann. Physik (Halle) 19 (1805):298–327.
Gilbert's extract of Davy's pp. 331–450.

J. chim. phys. 2 (an X):5–9.
Extracted from Ferriar's review.

Bull. sci. soc. philomathique 3 (1811):164–165 (frimaire, an XI).
A. F. de Fourcroy's report emphasizes the chemistry of nitrous oxide. (This volume has a typographical error in page numbering; reference is to the first set of pages numbered 100.)

T. *Chemische und physiologische Untersuchungen über das oxydirte Stickgas und das Athmen desselben. Aus dem englischen übersetzt.* Lemgo, Germ. 1812–14. 2 parts.
Cited in Bolton (not seen).

3.* An account of some experiments made with the galvanic apparatus of Signor Volta

J. Nat. Phil. Chem. Arts 4:275–281.

A. *Phil. Mag.* 7:347.
C. *Ann. Physik (Halle)* 7 (1801):114–131.

4.* Additional experiments on galvanic electricity

J. Nat. Phil. Chem. Arts 4:326–328.

Davy's letter was dated Dowry Square, Hotwells, 22 September 1800.

c. *Ann. Physik (Halle)* 7 (1801):114–131.
   See also 1800:3c.

5.* Notice of some observations on the causes of the galvanic phenomena, and on certain modes of increasing the powers of the galvanic pile of Volta

J. Nat. Phil. Chem. Arts 4:337–342.
Davy's corrections for this paper are on p. 402.

c. *Ann. Physik (Halle)* 8 (1801):1–21.
   See 1800:7c.

6.* Extract of a letter to Mr. Nicholson, dated Oct. 23, supplementary to his paper on galvanism in the present number

J. Nat. Phil. Chem. Arts 4:380–381.
The paper referred to is 1800:5.

c. *Ann. Physik (Halle)* 8 (1801):1–21
   See 1800:7c.

7.* An account of some additional experiments and observations on the galvanic phenomena

J. Nat. Phil. Chem. Arts 4:394–402.

c. *Ann. Physik (Halle)* 8 (1801):1–21, 300–315.
   Abstracted by Gilbert along with 1800:5 and 6 and 1801:1. He called for more experiments to decide whether chemical changes produce electrical ones, as Davy claimed.

8. [Concentration of nitrous (that is, nitric) acid suggested for use in the treatment of syphilis]

Communications respecting the external and internal use of nitrous acid; demonstrating its efficacy in every form of venereal disease, and extending its use to other complaints: with original facts, and a preliminary discourse, by the editor, Thomas Beddoes, M.D. London: printed for J. Johnson. Page 1 [fifty].
Beddoes's "Preliminary Discourse" set forth the claims of the East India practitioners that syphilis could be cured, either if the patient swallowed doses of diluted nitric acid, or if his legs were soaked in acid solutions. Davy's memo showed how acid of the suggested concentration could be prepared from commercially available acid.

9.   [Letter to Dr. Beddoes]

Communications respecting the external and internal use of nitrous acid; demonstrating its efficacy in every form of venereal disease, and extending its use to other complaints: with original facts, and a preliminary discourse, by the editor, Thomas Beddoes, M.D. London: printed for J. Johnson, pp. lviii–lix.

Davy's undated letter confirmed that one Charles Brown had not been at the Pneumatic Institution after April 1799, and that Brown had never examined any syphilitic patients while he was there. Before July 1799 all syphilitics at the Pneumatic Institution were treated with solutions of nitrous acid (see 1800:8); after that date some were treated with inhalations of oxygen and nitrous oxide gas.

1801

1.★ Letter from Mr. Davy, superintendent of the Pneumatic Institution containing notices concerning galvanism

J. Nat. Phil. Chem. Arts 4:527.
Davy's letter is dated Dowry Square, Hotwells, 23 January, 1801.

c. *Ann. Physik* (Halle) 8:300–315.
Abstracted by Gilbert. (See also 1800:7c.) His added notes explain differences in terminology between the German and British chemists.

2.★ An account of some galvanic combinations, formed by the arrangement of single metallic plates and fluids, analogous to the new galvanic apparatus of Mr. Volta. By Mr. Humphry Davy, lecturer on chemistry in the Royal Institution. Communicated by Benjamin Count of Rumford, V.P.R.S.

Phil. Trans. [91]:397–402.
Royal Society manuscript L & P XI. 167.
Read to the Royal Society on June 18.

r. *Phil. Mag.* 11:202–206.
J. Nat. Phil. Chem. Arts 5:341–344.
a. *Monthly Rev.* 37 (1802):297–298.
Reviewed by Charles Hatchett.
Phil. Mag. 10:85.
J. Nat. Phil. Chem. Arts 5:78.

T. *Ann. Physik (Halle)* 11 (1802):388–393.
   J. chim. phys. 2 (an X):261–268.
C. *Bibl. brit.* 17 (an IX):237–245.
   M. A. Pictet's report, first published here, was based on
   his notes taken at the Royal Society reading, on his inspection of the Voltaic apparatus at the Royal Institution,
   and on his conversations with Davy. He subsequently
   reprinted the report in *Voyage de trois mois en Angleterre,
   en Écosse, et en Irland, pendant l'été de l'an IX.* Geneva and
   Paris, an XI, p. 40f.

3. [Davy's first lecture course at the Royal Institution]

A. *Phil. Mag.* 9:281–282; 10:86–87.
   Davy's lecture series on galvanism began 25 April. See
   1801:5.

4.★ An account of a new eudiometer

   J. Royal Inst. 1:45–48.

R. *Repert. Arts Manufactures* 15:170–174.
   J. Nat. Phil. Chem. Arts 5:175–177; ns 1 (1802):41–44.
   Phil. Mag. 10:56–58.
T. *Allgem. J. Chem.* 8 (1802):86–93.
   Ann. Physik (Halle) 19 (1805):394–399.
   See also 1802:2T.
   J. chim. phys. 2 (an X):21–25.
C. *Ann. chim.* 42 (an X):301–304.
   Citoyen Guyton's abstract was critical of Davy's conclusion
   that the salubrity of air is independent of the proportions
   of the constituent parts.
   Bibl. brit. 17 (an IX):246–252.

5.★ The following outlines of a view of galvanism are chiefly
    extracted from a course of lectures on the galvanic pheno-
    mena, read at the theatre of the Royal Institution by Mr.
    Davy

   J. Royal Inst. 1 (1802):49–66.
   Davy's own abstract, dated 1 September 1801, contained
   the note (p. 53) that "Dry nitre, caustic potash, and soda
   are conductors of galvanism when rendered fluid by a
   high degree of heat; but the order of their conducting
   powers has not yet been ascertained." See also 1801:3.

R. *Phil. Mag.* 11:326–340.

6.   Outlines of observations relating to nitrous oxide, or dephlogisticated nitrous air

    J. Nat. Phil. Chem. Arts 5 (1801):281–287.
    "Extracted from 'Researches, Chemical and Philosophical, concerning Nitrous Oxide, 1800, Johnson,' with additions, and communicated by the author." See 1800:2.

1802

1.⋆ A syllabus of a course of lectures on chemistry delivered at the Royal Institution of Great Britain

    London, Royal Institution Press. 3 pp., l., 91 pp.
    Davy dated his "Advertisement" January 5.

A. *J. Nat. Phil. Chem. Arts* ns 1: 155.
    Monthly Rev. 39:428–429.
    Reviewed by Charles Hatchett.
G. *Allgem. J. Chem.* 9:342.
    The chief parts of the syllabus are listed in English.

2.   Note respecting the absorption of nitrous gas, by solutions of green sulphate and muriate of iron

    J. Nat. Phil. Chem. Arts ns 1:107-109.

T. *Allgem. J. Chem.* 10 (1803):104–105.
C. *Ann. Physik (Halle)* 19 (1805):394–399.

3.⋆ An account of a method of constructing simple and compound galvanic combinations, without the use of metallic substances and by means of charcoal and different fluids

    J. Royal Inst. 1:79–80.
    The paper is dated 9 January 1802.

R. *J. Nat. Phil. Chem. Arts* ns 1:144–145.
    Phil. Mag. 11:340–341.
T. *Ann Physik (Halle)* 11:394–395.
    J. chim. phys. 2 (an X):292–294.
C. *Bull sci. soc. philomathique* 3 (1811):111-112 (floréal, an X).
    Dr. Charles Blagden's letter to the Institute is published here. (The volume has a typographical error in pagination; the reference is to the first set of pages numbered 100.)

4.* A discourse, introductory to a course of lectures on chemistry, delivered in the theatre of the Royal Institution on the 21st of January, 1802
Sold at the house of the Royal Institution. London. 26 pp.

A. *Monthly Rev.* 39:428–429.
Reviewed by Charles Hatchett.

5. Mr. Davy's lectures on chemistry

J. Royal Inst. 1:109–112.
Davy's own summaries of his morning course (General chemistry) and his evening course (Outlines of chemical science, and the chemistry of the arts) for the series beginning 21 January and 7 February, respectively. Frederick Accum (*J. Nat. Phil. Chem. Arts* ns 1:295–296) described six spectacular experiments developed by Davy for use in these lectures.

A. *The notebooks of Samuel Taylor Coleridge*, vol. I, *1794–1804*. Kathleen Coburn, ed., New York: Bollingen Series L, Pantheon Books (1957), 1098 f 2–f 31v.
Coleridge attended Davy's first morning lecture of January 21. Miss Coburn does not think he attended the entire morning series; however his notes provide a complete summary of the series as Davy outlined them, so it may well be that Coleridge did attend them all. Davy had also given Coleridge an autographed copy of his *Syllabus*. (See 1802:1).

6. Observations on the acetous and acetic acid. By M. Darracq

J. Royal Inst. 1:132–133.
Davy's abstract of a paper published in *Ann. chim.* 41 (an X):264–281. John Sadler's glossary (see 1804:1) accepted Darracq's conclusion that acetous and acetic acid differed only in concentration and not composition.

7. Observations on gluten. By C. L. Cadet

J. Royal Inst. 1:133–134.
Davy's abstract of a paper in *Ann. chim.* 41 (an X):315–322.

8.* An account of some experiments on galvanic electricity, made in the theatre of the Royal Institution

J. Royal Inst. 1:165–167.

T. *Bibl. brit.* 20:318–322.

9.* An account of a method of copying paintings upon glass, and of making profiles, by the agency of light upon nitrate of silver. Invented by T. Wedgwood, Esq. With observations by H. Davy

J. Royal Inst. 1:170–174.

R. *J. Nat. Phil. Chem. Arts* ns 3:167–170.
T. *Ann. chim. storia naturale* 21:212–218.
Ann. Physik (Halle) 13 (1803):113–119.
Mag. naturvidensk. 4 (1824):23–28.
(Not seen.)
C. *Ann. chim.* 45 (an XI):256.
Abstracted by Berthollet.
J. Chem. Physik Mineral. 4 (1807):58–60.
Bull. sci. soc. philomathique 3 (an IX):167.

10. Discovery of two new gases. M. C. F. Bucholz

J. Royal Inst. 1:174–175.
Davy's abstract of *J. chim. phys.* 2 (an X):173–183. Bucholz claimed that when carbon was heated with barium carbonate, carbon monoxide and hydrogen cyanide were evolved. Nitrogen was said to have come from the barium carbonate. Davy commented that "when so important a discovery as that of the decomposition of a body before considered as simple is supposed to have been made, we have a right to expect the greatest precision and accuracy of experiment, and till they are attained, it is much better to doubt than to amuse ourselves with hopes that are too often vain."

11. Chemical examination of a new gas, composed of hydrogene, carbon, and phosphorous. By J. B. Trommsdorf

J. Royal Inst. 1:175–176.
Davy's critical abstract of *J. chim. phys.* 2 (an X):213–221, 225–233. Using the author's data, Davy produced another, equally acceptable theoretical composition for the gas J. B. Trommsdorf announced.

12. Experiments on charcoal. By Clement and Desormes

J. Royal Inst. 1:181–184.
Davy's abstract of *Ann. chim.* 42 (an X):121–152.

13.   Notice concerning the dilatation of aeriform fluids by heat.
      By M. Guay-Lussac [*sic*]

    J. Royal Inst. 1:196–197.
    Davy's brief abstract of *Ann. chim.* 43 (an X):137–175.

14.   [Letter to Pictet]

    Bibl. brit. 20 (an X):384–386.
    Davy's letter, dated Royal Institution, 21 July 1802,
    responded to Berthollet's criticism of Davy's determina-
    tion of the composition of nitrous oxide (see 1800:2C).
    Berthollet's subsequent rejoinder appeared in *Ann. chim.*
    44 (an XI):43–44. Davy's letter also served as introduction
    for 1802:15C.

15.★ Account of some experiments made in the laboratory of
      the Royal Institution, relating to the agencies of galvanic
      electricity, in producing heat, and in effecting changes in
      different fluid substances

    J. Royal Inst. 1:209–214.

  R. *J. Nat. Phil. Chem. Arts* ns 3:135–139, pl., ns 5:218.
  T. *Ann. chim.* 44 (an XI):206–216.
     Translated by Adet.
     Ann. Physik (Halle) 12 (1803):353–360.
  C. *Bibl. brit.* 20 (an X):386–393.
     For Davy's introduction see 1802:14C.

16.   On the change produced in carbonic acid gas by the electri-
      cal spark. By Theodore de Saussure

    J. Royal Inst. 1:217–218.
    Davy's abstract of *J. phys. chim. histoire nat. arts* 54 (an X):
    450–454.

17.   Note on a method of preserving animal substances from
      putrefaction. By Mr. Chaussier

    J. Royal Inst. 1:227.
    Davy's abstract of *Bull. soc. sci. philomathique* 3.3.

18.   Observations on the evaporation of water at a high tempera-
      ture. By Mr. Klaproth

    J. Royal Inst. 1:229–231.
    Davy's abstract of *J. phys. chim. histoire nat. arts* 55 (an X):

62–64. M. H. Klaproth hoped to confirm Leidenfrost's thesis (1756) that drops of water evaporate more slowly from an iron spoon at white heat than from one heated only to 212°F.

19. Observations on some phenomena produced in experiments made on the combination of iron with silver, and with lead. By Guyton

J. Royal Inst. 1:233–234.
Davy's abstract of *Ann. chim.* 43 (an X):47–55.

20. A continuation of an essay upon ether, containing some researches on a new state of the sulphuric acid, and upon some of its combinations. By Mr. Dabit

J. Royal Inst. 1:234–235.
Davy's abstract of *Ann. chim.* 43 (an X):101–112.

21. Experiments concerning the action of certain metals and earths lately discovered on the colouring matter of cochineal. By M. Hermstaedt [*sic*]

J. Royal Inst. 1:235–237.
Davy's abstract of Hermbstadt's paper in *J. chim. phys.* 2 (an X):240–248 complained that nothing was said of the degree of permanency of the colors produced. Davy concluded that the nature of the color depended upon the kind of acid used in the dyeing process.

22. Experiments on the colouring properties of the molybdic acid and on its use as a mordant. By M. D. Jaeger

J. Royal Inst. 1:237–239.
Davy's abstract of *J. chim. phys.* 2 (an X):253–260.

23. New experiments on artificial cold. By M. Lowitz

J. Royal Inst. 1:239–240.
Davy's abstract of *J. phys. chim.* 2 (an X):303–305.

24. An account of a composition for tinging oak and pear wood of a mahogany colour; and of a durable varnish for wood. By M. J. C. Danneman, Jr.

J. Royal Inst. 1:240.
Davy's abstract of *J. chim phys.* 2 (an X):321–322.

    A. *Monthly Mag.* 14 (1803):344.
        The notice mistakenly assumed that the process described
        had been originally proposed by Davy.

25.   Observations on the zoonic acid. By Thenard

    J. Royal Inst. 1:245–247.
    Davy's abstract of *Ann. chim.* 43 (an X):176–184.

26.   Chemical examination of the juice of the pawpaw

    J. Royal Inst. 1:247–249.
    Davy's abstract of a paper by N. Vauquelin, *Ann. chim.* 43
    (an X):267–275. Davy added that papaya juice makes
    tough meat tender.

27.   Extract, from a memoir by Mr. Ekeburg, on certain proper-
      ties of yttria, as compared with those of glucine; and upon
      two substances in which he has found a new metal

    J. Royal Inst. 1:249–253.
    Davy's translation of Vauquelin's extract in *Ann. chim.* 43
    (an X):276–283. Davy added notes to his own translation.
    Vauquelin's text was based on another translation by
    E. T. Swedenstierna.

28.   On the colcothar, used for polishing. By Guyton

    J. Royal Inst. 1:254.
    Davy's abstract of *Ann. chim.* 43 (an X):331–332.

29.   On the oxides of mercury, and on mercurial salts. By M.
      Fourcroy

    J. Royal Inst. 1:255–256.
    Davy's abstract of *J. Mines* 12 (an X):283–286.

30.   Extract of a letter from Mr. Pfaff

    J. Royal Inst. 1:260–261.
    Davy's translation of *J. phys. chim. histoire nat. arts* 55 (an X):
    235–236, which claimed that J. W. Ritter found the north
    pole of a magnetized iron wire oxidized more rapidly in
    water than did the south pole.

31.   Discovery of a comet. By Mechain

J. Royal Inst. 1:261.
Davy's abstract of *J. phys. chim. histoire nat. arts* 55 (an X): 237.

32.⋆ Observations on the appearances produced by the collision of steel with hard bodies

J. Royal Inst. 1:264–267.

R. *J. Nat. Phil. Chem. Arts* ns 4 (1803):103–106.
T. *Bibl. brit.* 22 (1803):335–342.
Ann. Physik (Halle) 17 (1804):446–452.
Presumed to have been translated by Gilbert; he was at least responsible for the added notes to the German literature.
Neues allgem. J. Chem. 1 (1803):371–376.
Translated by J. L. G. Meinecke.
C. *Ann. chim.* 46 (an XI):273–274.
Abstracted by Berthollet.

33.⋆ Account of a simple method of estimating the changes of volume produced in gases, by alterations of temperature, and of atmospheric pressure, in the course of chemical experiments

J. Royal Inst. 1:269–272.

R. *J. Nat. Phil. Chem. Arts* ns 4 (1803):32–34.
C. *Ann. Physik (Halle)* 16 (1804):104–109.
In his notes the editor, Gilbert, queried Davy's understanding of the gas laws, and called attention to his own work and that of A. Volta, Dalton, and Gay-Lussac as well.

34.⋆ Observations on different methods of obtaining gallic acid

J. Royal Inst. 1:273–275.

T. *Neues allgem J. Chem.* 1 (1803):567–569.
Translated by J. L. G. Meinecke; notes added by A. F. Gehlen.
C. *Ann. chim.* 52 (1804):21–22.
Bull. sci. soc. philomathique 3 (1811):166–167 (frimaire, an XI). Abstracted by Alexander Brongniart. (This volume has a typographical error in pagination; reference is to the first set of pages numbered 100.)

35. Description of a new process for refining gold. By Darcet, The Nephew

J. Royal Inst. 1:275–276.
  · Davy's abstract of *J. phys. chim. histoire nat. arts* 55 (an X): 259–263. Davy pointed out that the use of potassium nitrate as solvent, recommended by Darcet, usually resulted in some gold loss, as Smithson Tenant had established in *Phil. Trans.* [87] (1797):219–221.

36. Extract of a letter from Professor Proust to J. C. Delametherie concerning the discovery of a new metal

    J. Royal Inst. 1:276.
    Davy's abstract of *J. phys. chim. histoire nat. arts* 55 (an X): 297. "Silenium" had been found in a Hungarian lead ore.

37. Analysis of an ore of uranium. By M. Sage

    J. Royal Inst. 1:276–277.
    Davy's abstract of *J. phys. chim. histoire nat. arts* 55 (an X): 314–317.

38. Essay on the colours obtained from metallic oxides, capable of being fixed, by fusion, upon vitreous substances. By Alexander Brongniart, director of the porcelain manufactory at Sevres

    J. Royal Inst. 1:278–284.
    Davy's abstract of *J. Mines* 12 (an X):58–80.

39.★ Observations relating to the progress of galvanism

    J. Royal Inst. 1:284–290.
    Davy surveyed the literature and took issue with Guyton's results, reported in *Mag. encyclopédique*, an XI.

40. On the preparation of phosphuret of lime

    J. Royal Inst. 1:294–295.
    J. B. Van Mons described a method of preparation for phosphuret of lime in *J. chim. phys.* 3 (an X):75–77, which Davy theorized was too costly. W. Clayfield's modification of an older process of G. Pearson was more advantageous. Lime should be heated to redness before the phosphorus is distilled over it, to reduce the loss of phosphorous. Davy pointed out the procedure also works well with strontium and barium salts.

41. New observations on the conversion of fixed oils into wax. By Brugnatelli

J. Royal Inst. 1:295.
Davy's abstract of *J. chim. phys.* 3 (an X):70–72.

42. Extract of a letter from the counsellor Westrumb, concerning the discovery of two new principles in sulphureted waters

J. Royal Inst. 1:295–296.
Davy's abstract of *J. chim. phys.* 3 (an XI):113–114.

43. Extract of a letter from M. C. Gimbernat, concerning the discovery of a new gas (sulphureted nitrogene gas) in the mineral waters at Aix-la-Chapelle

J. Royal Inst. 1:296.
Davy's abstract of *J. chim. phys.* 3 (an XI):114–115.

44. [Summary of a paper by Richard Chenevix on the humors of the eye, read to the Royal Society on 4 November 1802]

J. Royal Inst. 1:296–298.
Davy's summary of a paper eventually published in *Phil. Trans.* [93] (1803):195–199.

45. [Summary of a paper by James Smithson, on the chemical analysis of some calamines, read to the Royal Society on 18 November 1802]

J. Royal Inst. 1:299–302.
Davy's summary of a paper eventually published in *Phil. Trans.* [93] (1803):12–28.

46. Extract from a memoir on the sap of vegetables. By Vauquelin

J. Royal Inst. 1:302–306.
Davy's abstract of an account of Vauquelin's work by Citoyen Tassaert in *Ann. chim.* 31 (1798):20–40. He called attention to the paper even though it was no longer new, for it "could not fail to throw considerable light upon the phenomena of vegetation."

47.⋆ An account of a method of obtaining the salts of iron at the minimum of oxidation

J. Royal Inst. 1:308–309.

R. *Phil. Mag.* 14 (1803):373–374.

   T. *Neues allgem. J. Chem.* 1 (1803):106–107.
      Translated by Meinecke.

   C. *Bull. sci. soc. philomathique* 3 (1811):173–174 (nivoise, an XI).
      (The volume has an error in pagination; reference is to
      the first set of pages numbered 100.)

48. [Summary of a paper by G. Aldini on galvanism, read to
    the Royal Society on 25 November 1802]

    J. Royal Inst. 1:310–311.
      Davy's summary of a paper eventually published in *Ann.
      Physik (Halle)* 14 (1803):320–339.

49. Letter from T. C. De Saussure, on the supposed decomposi-
    tion of the gaseous oxide of carbon, by hydrogene gas

    J. Royal Inst. 1:313–314.
      Davy's abstract critical of *J. phys. chim. histoire nat. arts* 55
      (an X):396.

50. Note on the influence of galvanism on the fibrine of the
    blood. By G. F. Circaud

    J. Royal Inst. 1:314.
      Davy's abstract of *J. phys. chim. histoire nat. arts* 55 (an X):
      402–403.

51.* Some observations upon the motions of small pieces of
    acetite of potash, during their solution, upon the surface of
    water.

    J. Royal Inst. 1:314–315.

52. Observations on M. Berthollet's memoirs on charcoal, and
    on the hydrocarbonates

    J. Royal Inst. 1:315–318.

1803

1. Outlines of a course of lectures on the chemistry of agricul-
    ture to be delivered before the board of agriculture, 1803

    London, printed by B. McMillan. Bow-Street, Covent
    Garden. 14 pp.
      Copy in John Fulton's Collection, Yale University Medical
      Library.

2.★ An account of some experiments and observations on the constituent parts of certain astringent vegetables; and on their operation in tanning

> *Phil. Trans.* [93]:233–273.
> Issued separately, London: W. Bulmer, 41 pp.
> Royal Society manuscript L & P XII. 48.
> Read to the Royal Society 24 February.

R. *Phil. Mag.* 17:63–76, 212–217, 295–304.
> *J. Nat. Phil. Chem. Arts* ns 5:256–276; 6:31–41.

A. *Phil. Mag.* 15:181–182.
> *Monthly Rev.* 42:409–413.
> Reviewed by John Yellowly.
> For Davy's own abstract see 1803:3.

T. *Annales des Arts* 18 (an XII):54–82, 136–168.
> (Not seen.)
> *Bibl. brit.* 26 (an XII):158–172.
> Translated by C. G. De la Rive.

C. *Neues allgem. J. Chem.* 4 (1805):343–382.
> Reported by Gehlen, who based it on both items in T above: the added footnotes are his.

3. An account of some experiments and observations on the constituent parts of certain astringent vegetables, and on their operation in tanning

> *J. Royal Inst.* 2:65–70.
> Davy's own abstract.

4. Essay on the fecula of green plants. By Professor Proust

> *J. Royal Inst.* 2:26.
> Davy's abstract of *J. phys chim. histoire nat. arts* 56 (an XI): 97–118.

5. Extract of a letter from Dr. Bremen of Berlin, to M. Friedlander, on the prussic acid contained in certain plants

> *J. Royal Inst.* 2:26–27.
> Davy's abstract of *J. phys. chim. histoire nat. arts* 56 (an XI).

6. Experiments on the stones said to have fallen from above. By M. Vauquelin

> *J. Royal Inst.* 2:27.
> Davy's abstract of *Ann. chim.* 45 (1802):225–245.

7.   Extract of a letter from Dr. Carbonell, a Spanish physician, to Mr. Deyeux, on a new method of making a stone-colour pigment unalterable by air

    J. Royal Inst. 2:27.
    Davy's abstract of *Ann. chim.* 45 (1802):257.

8.   Experiments on the absorption of different gases by water, at different temperatures, and under different pressures. By William Henry. Communicated by the President of the Royal Society. Read 23 December 1802

    J. Royal Inst. 2:28–29.
    Davy's abstract of a paper subsequently printed in *Phil. Trans.* [93] (1803):29–42, 274–276.

9.★ Observations on the processes of tanning

    J. Royal Inst. 2:30–38.

R. *Phil. Mag.* 16:82–85; 17:58–62.

10.   Experiments and observation on the various alloys,—on the specific gravity,—and on the comparative wear of gold —being the substance of a report made to the right honour-able the Lords of the Committee of Privy Council, appointed to take into consideration the state of the coins of this kingdom, and the present establishment and constitution of his Majesty's mint. By Charles Hatchett, Esq. F.R.S. Read to the Royal Society January 13, 1803

    J. Royal Inst. 2:47–62.
    Davy's abstract of a paper subsequently published in *Phil Trans.* [93] (1803):43–194.

11.   An account of some experiments on gunpowder. By Benjamin Roebuck, Esq. of Madras. Communicated by James Watt, Esq. F.R.S. Read to the Royal Society March 31, 1803

    J. Royal Inst. 2:71.
    Davy's abstract of a paper not published by the Royal Society.

12.   Inquiries concerning the nature of a metallic substance lately sold in London as a new metal, under the title of palladium. By R. Chenevix, Esq. F.R.S. and M.R.I.A. Read to the Royal Society May 12, 1803

J. Royal Inst. 2:76–78.
Davy's abstract of a paper subsequently published in *Phil. Trans.* [93] (1803):290–320.

13[?]. Aldini on galvanism

Edin. Rev. 3:194–198.
Wellesley Index suggests that this review may have been written by Davy, or that he may have been associated with it. (For Davy's interest in Aldini's work see 1802:48.) Another possible author is John Thomson.

1804

1.★ Outlines of a course of lectures on chemical philosophy

London, from the press of the Royal Institution of Great Britain, Albemarle Street: W. Savage, Printer. 3 pp. l., [3]–54 pp. 20 cm.
Designed to accompany Davy's text was John Sadler's (Chemical Operator to the Royal Institution) *An explanation of terms used in chemistry*, London: Royal Institution, 22 pp.

{2.★} [Of Pliny the Elder]

Works, VII, 120–121.
An extract from Davy's lecture series.

{3.★} [Of Lord Bacon]

Works, VII, 121–122.
An extract from Davy's lecture series.

{4.★} [Of the Elder Bacon]

Works, VII, 122–123.
An extract from Davy's lecture series.

5. [Analysis of a lead ore]

General view of the agriculture of the county of Caithness, by John Henderson. London, 1812, pp. 337–340. "Copy of an advertisement, regarding a lead mine discovered in the hill of Skinnet, the property of Sir John Sinclair, Bart."
Davy's undated analysis of lead ore appears on p. 338, and forms part of the addenda to the advertisement of 20 November.

1805

1. Prologue. (Written by a friend)

   The honey moon: A comedy, in five acts. As performed at the Theatre-Royal, Drury-Lane, with universal applause. A new edition. By the late John Tobin, Esq. Printed for Longmans, Hurst, Rees, and Orme, Paternoster-Row, By T. Davison, Whitefriars, pp. [7–8].

   > Davy is identified as the author in *Life*, I, 184. With the cooperation of one of the Sothebys, he wrote the prologue in a few hours the day before the play opened. The prologue was spoken on opening night by one Mr. Bartley.

   R. Another edition.

   > Philadelphia: Printed for E. Bronson, at the Office of the United States' Gazette, pp. [3–4].

2.★ An account of some analytical experiments on a mineral production from Devonshire, consisting principally of alumine and water

   Phil. Trans. [95]:155–162.
   Royal Society manuscript L & P XII.92.
   > Read to the Royal Society 28 February.

   R. *Phil. Mag.* 22:35–40.
   J. Nat. Phil. Chem. Arts 11:153–158.
   A. *Monthly Mag.* 19:576.
   Monthly Rev. 48:262.
   > Reviewed by John Bostock.
   T. *Ann. chim.* 60 (1806):297–309.

3.★ On a method of analysing stones containing fixed alkali, by means of the boracic acid

   Phil. Trans. [95]:231–232.
   Royal Society manuscript L & P XII.102.
   > Read to the Royal Society 16 May.

   R. *J. Nat. Phil. Chem. Arts* 13 (1806):86–87.
   Phil. Mag. 23 (1806):146–147.
   A. *Monthly Rev.* 49 (1806):388.
   > Reviewed by John Bostock.
   T. *J. Chem. Physik Mineral.* 1 (1806):151–152.
   C. *Ann. chim.* 55:84–86.

4. On the analysis of soils, as connected with their improvement

Communications to the Board of Agriculture 4:302–318.

R. *J. Nat. Phil. Chem. Arts* 12:81–97.
Issued separately, W. Bulmer.
Phil. Mag. 23 (1806):26–41.
Agricultural Museum 1 (1811):235–239, 252–256, 264–269, 273–279.
A. *Monthly Rev.* 51 (1806):370.
Reviewed by Christopher Moody.
T. *J. Chem. Physik Mineral.* 2 (1806):345–363.

{5.⋆} Introductory lecture for the courses of 1805

Works, VIII, 155–166.
John Davy stated that this lecture introduced all of the lectures to be delivered at the Royal Institution for the season.

1806

1. [Letter to Mr. Nicholson]

J. Nat. Phil. Chem. Arts 14:267.
Davy's letter, dated Killarney, Ireland, 15 June, announced that wavellite contains fluoric acid.

T. *Ann. Physik (Halle)* 24:119–120.

{2.⋆} [Journal of a tour in Ireland]

Works, VII, 146–165.
Davy's entries are dated from 27 June to 24 July.

3.⋆ The Bakerian lecture, on some chemical agencies of electricity

Phil. Trans. [97]:1–56 + pl.
Royal Society manuscript, PT. 1. 2.
Davy's first Bakerian lecture, read to the Royal Society 20 November. For the paper Davy was awarded Napoleon's prize of 3000 francs in the gift of the French Institute.

R. *Phil. Mag.* 28 (1807):3–18, 104–119, 220–233, + pl.
J. Nat. Phil. Chem. Arts supp 18 (1807):321–339; 19 (1808): 37–63.

Experimental researches in chemistry, Glasgow: Griffin, 1842 (Griffin's scientific miscellany, pt. 8), pp. 1–22.

A. *J. Nat. Phil. Chem. Arts* 16 (1807):79–80.

Phil. Mag. 26:181, 266, 269.

Edin. Rev. 11 (1807):390–398.

Reviewed by Henry Brougham.

Monthly Mag. 25 (1808, pt. I):58–59.

Monthly Rev. 54 (1807):1–4.

Reviewed by Bostock.

T. *Bibl. brit.* 34 (1807):397–400; 35 (1807):16–59, 141–184.

Translation presumed to be by Pictet.

Ann. chim. 63 (1807):172–224, 225–266.

Translated by Berthollet.

J. Chem. Physik Mineral. 5 (1808):9–58.

C. H. Pfaff's retranslation of Berthollet's text.

"Electrochemische Untersuchungen Vorgelesen als Bakerian Lecture am 20. November 1806 und am 19. November 1807." Ludwig W. Gilbert, trans., Leipzig, 1893, 92 pp. (*Ostwald's Klassiker der exacten Wissenschaften.* No. 45). (See 1807:6T.)

C. *J. phys. chim. histoire nat. arts* 64 (1807):421–461.

Ann. Physik (Halle) 28 (1808):1–43, 161–202.

A review by Gilbert initially based on that by DelaMétherie. When Gilbert received the translation in *Bibl. brit.*, however, and that by Berthollet, he improved the first section of his translation on pp. 155–159. Gilbert's comments on pile action are collected on pp. 203–222. The second section of the translation (pp. 161–202) was based on both Pictet's and Berthollet's texts.

J. Chem. Physik Mineral. 3 (1807):169–170.

Translation of the abstract in *J. Nat. Phil. Chem. Arts.*

J. Chem. Physik Mineral. 4 (1807):274–279.

Reviewed by J. S. C. Schweigger. His comments related Davy's identification of chemical activity with galvanic action to early work by Ritter.

Bull. sci. soc. philomathique ns 1 (1807):71–76, 97–100, 105–110.

Abstracted by J. L. Gay-Lussac.

1807

{1.*} Introductory lecture to the chemistry of nature

Works, VIII, 167–179.

Davy's lecture written on 30 January for delivery on 31 January.

{2.★} [On the chemical composition of the atmosphere]

> *Works*, VIII, 239–255.
> Part of Davy's lecture series, "The chemistry of nature."

3.   On the causes that affected the progress of antient art

> *Director* 1:33–46.
> The first contributed essay in the journal, signed "Y."

4.   On the Gaelic poems of Ireland

> *Director* 1:321–329.
> An essay signed "V."

5.★ Parallels between art and science

> *Director* 2:193–198.
> An essay signed "A."

> 1807: 3, 4, and 5 were obliquely identified as having been written by Davy in the final essay of this short-lived journal, "Discovery of the authors of the foregoing essays," 2:367–382. Davy is positively identified as the author in T. F. Dibdin's *Reminiscences of a literary life*, 2 vols., John Major: London, 1836, I, 249–253.

6.★ The Bakerian lecture, on some new phenomena of chemical changes produced by electricity, particularly the decomposition of the fixed alkalies, and the exhibition of the new substances which constitute their bases; and on the general nature of alkaline bodies

> *Phil. Trans.* [98] (1808):1–44.
> Issued separately, London: W. Bulmer, 1808, 44 pp.
> Royal Society manuscript PT. 2. 1.
>
> > Davy's second Bakerian lecture, read to the Royal Society 19 November.

> R. *J. Nat. Phil. Chem. Arts* 20 (1808):290–314, supp. 20 (1808): 321–332.
> *Phil. Mag.* 32 (1808):3–18, 100–112, 146–154.
> *Experimental researches in chemistry*, Glasgow: Richard Griffin, 1842 (Griffin's scientific miscellany, pt. 8), pp. 23–40.
> *The decomposition of the fixed alkalies and alkaline earths ... 1807–1808*, Edinburgh: William F. Clay; London: Simpkin, Marshall, Hamilton, Kent, 1894 (Alembic club reprint, no. 6).

A. *Phil. Mag.* 29:180–181.

Pages 373–374 correct substantive errors in this early report.

J. Nat. Phil. Chem. Arts 19 (1808):78–79.

"A Chemist" corrected the errors in reporting, pp. 147–149.

Edin. Rev. 12 (1808):394–401.

Reviewed by Henry Brougham.

Ann. Phil. 5 (1815):1–9.

Monthly Repository 3 (1808):574.

Davy's discoveries were reported in America by Blagden to Benjamin Silliman.

Monthly Rev. 57:225–227.

Reviewed by John Bostock.

T. *Bibl. brit.* 39 (1808):3–69.

Ann. chim. 68 (1808):203–224, 225–276.

Reprinted from *Bibl. brit.*

J. phys. chim. histoire nat. arts 67 (1808):337–372.

J. Chem. Physik Mineral. 7 (1808):595–643.

Gehlen's translation from the French of *Bibl. brit.*, above. He pointed out that he added no comments.

Ann. Physik (Halle) 31 (1809): 113–175; 32 (1809): 245–267.

Translated by Gilbert.

C. *Bibl. brit.* 34:391–393.

Translation of a letter dated 23 November reporting on the Royal Society reading.

Ann. chim. 64:319–320.

Extract of a letter dated London, 23 November.

Bibl. brit. 37 (1808):180–186.

Copious translated extracts printed in response to a letter from Boissier (*ibid.*, 65–68) that Davy's work had been confirmed by Pictet and others and that they were impatiently waiting for a full report of Davy's work. Baron Jacquin's group in Vienna supplied additional confirmation for the decomposition of the alkalies (*ibid.*, 241–244).

J. phys. chim. histoire nat. arts 66 (1808):237–259.

Weiss [?] traced the route of communication of Davy's results to Munich.

J. phys. chim. histoire nat. arts 66:259–260.

DelaMétherie's translation from Nicholson's *Journal*, above. He further reviewed the work in 68 (1809):79–87.

J. Chem. Physik Mineral. 4 (1807):660–661.

A. F. Gehlen's abstract based on the letter in *Bibl. brit.*

J. Chem. Physik Mineral. 5 (1808):565–567, 567–570.

Gehlen's review of DelaMétherie's 1808 abstract, *J. phys. chem. histoire nat. arts* 67 (1808):337–372.

Ann. Physik (Halle) 27:117–120; 30 (1808):369–377; 31 (1809): 114n.

Translated by Gilbert from *Bibl. brit.* (1808). He noted that there seemed to be substantive differences between the initial reports of the reading of the paper as presented by *Bibl. brit.* and by DelaMétherie. In the 1809 section Gilbert pointed out the specific discrepancies between this early report and the published version in *Phil. Trans.*

Bull. sci. soc. philomathique ns 1:83–84, 110; (1808):237–241.

Abstracted by Gay-Lussac from a letter reporting the reading to the Royal Society. The second report (1808) was based on a reprint of the original paper.

7.   [Lettter to Rev. James Hall]

R. *Phil. Mag.* 35 (1810):180–186.

Ann. Register 51 (1809) [1821]:866.

Both reprints were made from *Trans. Soc. Arts Manuf. Comm.* (1809) (not seen). Davy's undated letter described the bleachability of a hemplike substance which Hall had made from bean stalks. Davy's letter had formed part of Hall's certificates submitted to the Society for the Encouragement of Arts, for their Silver Medal. Joseph Hume on 24 February also reported on his attempts at bleaching the fiber; the date for Davy's report has been taken from that.

1808

{1.⋆} Lecture I.—Introductory to electrochemical science

Works, VIII, 274–286.

Davy opened his series on 12 March, after he had recovered from a serious illness.

{2.⋆} Lecture II.—Electro-chemical science

Works, VIII, 287–305.

3.⋆ Electro-chemical researches, on the decomposition of the earths; with observations on the metals obtained from the alkaline earths, and on the amalgam procured from ammonia

Phil. Trans. [98]:333–370.
Issued separately, London: W. Bulmer, 38 pp.
Royal Society manuscript PT. 2.23.
    Read to the Royal Society 30 June.

R. *Phil. Mag.* 32:193–223.
J. Nat. Phil. Chem. Arts 21:368–383; 22 (1809):54–68.
Experimental researches in chemistry, Glasgow: Richard Griffin, 1842 (Griffin's scientific miscellany, pt. 8), pp. 41–56.
The decomposition of the fixed alkalies and alkaline earths ... 1807–1808, Edinburgh: William F. Clay; London: Simpkin, Marshall, Hamilton, Kent, 1894, pp. 46–51 (Alembic club reprints, no. 6).

A. *Edin. Rev.* 13 (1808–1809):462–469.
    Reviewed by Henry Brougham.
J. Nat. Phil. Chem. Arts 21:159.
Phil. Mag. 31:148–150.
Monthly Rev. 59 (1809):275–276.
    Reviewed by John Bostock.

T. *Ann. chim.* 70 (1809):189–223, 227–254.
    Translated by C. A. Prieur from Davy's "rough draft." Davy subsequently (1809:9) deplored the publication of his manuscript note (p. 250). He also corrected De la Rive's translations on pp. 240, 241, and 251.
J. Chem. Physik Mineral. 9 (1810):484–527.
    Gehlen's translation of Prieur, above. Gilbert appended his comments and queries on pp. 528–531.
Jahrb. Chem. Physik 1 (1811):300–324, 473–483; 2 (1811):42–63; 3 (1811):79–92.
    Pfaff continued Gehlen's translation from *Phil. Trans.* The notes were added by Gehlen.
Ann. Physik (Halle) 32 (1809):365–396.
    Translated by Gilbert directly from *Phil. Trans.* plus the note (p. 385) Davy sent to Prieur.
Ann. Physik (Halle) 33 (1809):267–274.
    Gilbert's translation of Davy's final footnote, which Gilbert called an appendix. Pages 273–274 contain a translation of a note, in Davy's hand, added to an offprint of the original paper. (See 1809:9).

C. *Bibl. brit.* 39:69–70.
    An unsigned letter from London in June, reporting Davy's work, but urging consideration of the alkaline metals as hydrides.
Ann. Physik (Halle) 31 (1809):176–177.
    Translated by Gilbert from *Bibl. brit.*, above.

Bibl. brit. 41 (1809):33–40, 115–138.
Pictet's long extract is based on a manuscript Davy sent
to him; a translation of Davy's letter of transmittal for
the paper, written 1 July, appears as a note (pp. 33–34).
J. Chem. Physik Mineral. 7:643–644.
Gehlen's translation of the unsigned letter in *Bibl. brit.*
above.
J. phys. chim. histoire nat. arts 66:105; 68 (1809):79–87.
DelaMétherie's brief report.
J. phys. chim. histoire nat. arts 68 (1809):468–476; 69 (1809):
78–90.
DelaMétherie's full abstract.
Bull. sci. soc. philomathique 1808, pp. 220–221.
A. M. C. Dumeril's extract from a letter by Blagden
reporting the Royal Society reading.

4.   [The concluding lectures at the Royal Institution]

A.   *Monthly Mag.* 25:537–539.
Abstract of Davy's lectures, emphasizing the experiments
Davy performed to demonstrate the decomposition of
the alkalies.

5.   [Letter to Benjamin Tucker]

*Report of the Surveyor-General of the Duchy of Cornwall to His
Royal Highness The Prince of Wales, concerning the obstacles,
facilities, and expence, attending the formation of a safe and
capacious roadstead with the Islands of Scilly,* B. Tucker: London; Sherwood, Neely, and Jones, 1810, pp. 33–34.
Davy's letter, dated 4 December 1808, reported his
analysis of lake water from the Scilly Isles.

6.★ The Bakerian Lecture. An account of some new analytical
researches on the nature of certain bodies, particularly the
alkalies, phosphorus, sulphur, carbonaceous matter, and
the acids hitherto undecompounded; with some general
observations on chemical theory

Phil. Trans. [99] (1809):39–104 +- pl.
Issued separately, London: W. Bulmer, 1809, 66 pp.
Royal Society manuscript PT. 3.3.
Davy's third Bakerian lecture, read to the Royal Society
15 December.

R.   *Phil. Mag.* 33 (1809):479–488; 34 (1809):6–19, 108–124, 181–
190, + pl.

J. Nat. Phil. Chem. Arts 23 (1809):241–257, 321–334; 24 (1809): 12–24, 95–105.

The elementary nature of chlorine . . . *1809–1818*, Edinburgh: William F. Clay; London: Simpkin, Marshall, Hamilton, Kent, 1894, pp. 5–17 (Alembic club reprint, no. 9).
    Reprint of Davy's pp. 39, 40, 91–103.

A. *J. Nat. Phil. Chem. Arts* 22 (1809):238–239.

Phil. Mag. 32:367–369.

Edin. Rev. 14 (1809):483–490.
    Reviewed by Henry Brougham.

Monthly Rev. 60 (1809):356–359.
    Reviewed by John Bostock.

T. *J. phys. chim. histoire nat. arts* 69 (1809):360–412 + pl.

Ann. Physik (Halle) 35 (1810):149–178, 278–291, 433–476.
    Translated by Gilbert directly from *Phil. Trans.*, with the help of the translation in *J. phys. chim. histoire nat. arts*. Gilbert supplied an appendix (pp. 477–478) reviewing Davy's publications beginning in 1806.

C. *Bibl. brit.* 41 (1809):99–104; 42 (1809):27–46, 113–140.
    De la Rive's added notes, signed "D.," appear throughout this commentary; these notes point out the "correct" views of Gay-Lussac and L. J. Thenard.

J. Chem. Physik Mineral. 9 (1810):533–537.

Ann. chim. 72 (1809):244–264; 73 (1810):1–35.
    De la Rive's abstract reprinted from *Bibl. brit.*, above.

1809

1.* New analytical researches on the nature of certain bodies, being an appendix to the Bakerian lecture for 1808

Phil. Trans. [99]:450–470.
Issued separately, W. Bulmer, 1809.
Royal Society manuscript PT. 3.28.
    Read to the Royal Society 2 February.

R. *Phil. Mag.* 34:339–347, 405–411.

J. Nat. Phil. Chem. Arts 25 (1810):136–151.

The elementary nature of chlorine . . . *1809–1818*. Edinburgh: William F. Clay; London: Simpkin, Marshall, Hamilton, Kent, 1894, pp. 18–20 (Alembic club reprint, no. 9).
    Reprint of Davy's pp. 468–470.

A. *Phil. Mag.* 33: 88–90, 173.

J. Nat. Phil. Chem. Arts 22:238–239.

        Monthly Rev. 62 (1810):56–57.
        Reviewed by John Bostock.
   c. *Bibl. brit.* 44 (1810):42–55.
        De la Rive's long extract, with notes by him to point out
        the "correct" views of Gay-Lussac and Thenard. Errors
        in the report are corrected on pp. 126–127.
        Ann. Physik (Halle) 36 (1810):180–190.
        Extracted by Gilbert from De la Rive's report, above. See
        also 1810:1.
        Jahrb. Chem. Physik 1 (1811):324–328, 484–488; 3 (1811):93–95.
        Gehlen's translation of De la Rive, above. Gehlen added
        his translations of Davy's letter (19 Jan. 1810) to Pictet
        in 1:328 (see 1810:1) and of one (9 Nov. 1809) to Prieur
        in 1:330–331 (see 1809:9).

   2. [Letter to Mr. Nicholson]

        J. Nat. Phil. Chem. Arts 22:150–151.
        Davy's reply to the queries of "G.K.M." about the
        design and construction of galvanic batteries.

   T. *Ann. Physik (Halle)* 35 (1810):479–481.
        Bibl. brit. 41:140–142.

{3.*} [Extract from an introductory lecture on electrochemistry,
expressing gratitude for the new battery at the Royal
Institution]

        Works, VIII, 355–359.

{4.*} [Extract from a lecture, in praise of experimental work]

        Works, VIII, 351.

{5.*} [Extract from a lecture on the relation between chemical
and electrical action]

        Works, VIII, 344–349.

{6.*} [Extract from a lecture, on the pursuit of knowledge]

        Works, VIII, 351.

{7.*} [Extract from a lecture, on the beneficial value of doubt]

        Works, VIII, 351–352.

{8.*} [Extract from a lecture, speculations on the compound
nature of nitrogen]

        Works, VIII, 323–328.

9.   [Letter to C. A. Prieur]

   T. *Ann. chim.* 74 (1810):215–219.
       Davy's letter, dated 9 November 1809, of which a portion
       was translated here, reported that his experimental work
       argued against considering potassium as an hydride.
       Corrections appear for 70 (1809):189–223, 227–254.
       Jahrb. Chem. Physik 1 (1811):330–331.
       Ann. Physik (Halle) 36 (1810):195–197.

10. Sketch of a plan for improving the Royal Institution, and
     erecting it on a permanent foundation

     Annual Register 51:822–826.
       Bence-Jones, pp. 285–288, believes that this statement
       about the Royal Institution, which was based on and
       quoted from a report of the Managers to the Visitors of
       20 March 1809, was written by Davy. See 1810:2.

11.* The Bakerian lecture for 1809. On some new electrochemi-
      cal researches, on various objects, particularly the metallic
      bodies, from the alkalies, and earths, and on some combina-
      tions of hydrogene

     Phil. Trans. [100] (1800):16–74 + 2 pl.
     Royal Society manuscript PT. 4.2.
       Davy's fourth Bakerian lecture, read to the Royal Society
       16 November.

   R. *Phil. Mag.* 35 (1810):401–415; 36:17–32, 85–96 + pl.
       J. Nat. Phil. Chem. Arts, supp. 26 (1810):321–339; 27 (1810):
       38–55, 99–111.
       The elementary nature of chlorine . . . 1809–1818. Edinburgh:
       William F. Clay; London: Simpkin, Marshall, Hamilton,
       Kent, 1894, pp. 20–21 (Alembic club reprint, no. 9).
         Reprint of Davy's p. 67
   A. *Phil. Mag.* 34:393.
       Monthly Mag. 30 (1810):350–353, 439–442, 542–545.
       Monthly Rev. 63 (1810):265–268.
         Reviewed by John Bostock.
   T. *J. phys. chim. histoire nat. arts* 71 (1810):43–61, 85–115.
       Translated by DelaMétherie. Davy's letter of transmittal
       appears as a note on pp. 43–44. See also 1810:13.
       Ann. chim. 75 (1810):27–77, 129–175.
         Translated by Prieur.
       Jahrb. Chem. Physik 3 (1811):334–352; 4 (1812):309–341 + pl.;
       5 (1812):354–363.

Schweigger's pastiche of several papers. He added his own comments and changed the order of Davy's sections. The notes on pp. 311 and 316, for example, contain the description of apparatus which originally appeared at the end of Davy's paper. (Page 309 of vol. 4 is incorrectly numbered 209.) See also 1810:13T.

Ann. Physik (Halle) 37 (1811):34–63, 155–207.
Translated by Gilbert from *Phil. Trans.* He found errors in Prieur's and DelaMétherie's translations.

C. *Bibl. brit.* 43 (1810):285–287, 288–290.
J. phys. chim. histoire nat. arts 27 (1810):341–343.
Ann. Physik (Halle) 36 (1810):281–284.
Gilbert prepared this interim report while working on the full translation.

1810

1. [Letter to the editor]

T. *Bibl. brit.* 43:192.
Davy's letter, dated 19 January, claimed that potassium cannot be decomposed by ammonia. The editor deplored Davy's brevity.
Ann. Physik (Halle) 36:191–195.
Gilbert noted that Davy had included the same material in a handwritten note in the reprint of 1809:1 (see 1809: 9) which he sent to Paris.
J. phys. chim. histoire nat. arts 71:348.

2. A Lecture on the plan which it is proposed to adopt for improving the Royal Institution, and rendering it permanent. Delivered in the theatre of the Royal Institution, March 3, 1810. Printed by desire of the Managers. 41 pp.

First lecture of Davy's second course of the season on electrochemistry. See 1809:10.

R. *Proc. Roy. Inst. G. Brit.* 21 (1914–1916):1–16.
Printed as a supplement to the volume.
A. *Phil. Mag.* 35:225–229.

{3.*} [Of Mr. Cavendish]

Works, VII, 127–137.

Extract from Davy's lecture of 17 March, in praise of Henry Cavendish.

A. *Phil. Mag.* 35:229–230.

{4.*} [Sketch of the character of Dr. J. Priestley]

Works, VII, 115–117.
Extract from Davy's lecture series.

{5.*} [Of Karl Wilhelm Scheele]

Works, VII, 118–120.
Extract from Davy's lecture series.

{6.*} [Historical sketch of electrical discovery]

Works, VIII, 256–273.
Extracted from Davy's lecture on electrochemical science.

{7.*} [Extract from a lecture, on the nature of heat]

Works, VIII, 349–350.

{8.*} [Extract from a lecture, on the unknown nature of heat]

Works, VIII, 350.

{9.*} [Extract from a lecture, on the use of chemical processes in manufacturing]

Works, VIII, 360–361.

10. Report to the Committee of the honourable House of Commons, on the petition of the Trustees of The British Museum; respecting the purchase of Mr. Greville's collection of minerals

Parl. pap. 258 (1810):11, 239.
In addition to Davy, the committee members were: William Babington, L. Compte De Bournon, Richard Chenevix, Robert Ferguson, Charles Hatchett, and William Hyde Wollaston. The report, signed on 9 May, covered the work of the committee from 2–9 May, and recommended that the collection be bought for £13,727.

11. Observations sur les recherches de MM. Gay-Lussac et Thenard, relativement a l'amalgame de l'ammoniaque

T. *J. phys. chim. histoire nat. arts* 70:389–392.
   Bibl. brit. 45:26–32.
   The editor stated that this paper and the two following
   (1810:12, 13) were received in MS from Davy. Extreme
   care was taken to provide accurate translations.
R. *Ann. chim.* 75:256–263.

12. Examen de quelques observations de MM. Gay-Lussac et
    Thenard, sur des faits relatifs aux métaux provenans des
    alkalis, insérées au Journal de Physique, déc. 1809, p. 455

T. *J. phys. chim. histoire nat. arts* 70:393–397.
   Bibl. brit. 45:33–40.
R. *Ann. chim.* 75:264–273.
T.' *Jahrb. Chem. Physik* 1 (1811):338–342.
   Translated by Gehlen, who added notes.

13. Réplique á la réponse aux recherches analytiques, etc.
    Journal de Physique Décembre 1809. Par MM Gay-Lussac
    et Thenard

T. *J. phys. chim. histoire nat. arts* 70:398–405.
   Bibl. brit. 45:120–132.
R. *Ann. chim.* 75:274–289.
T.' *Jahrb. Chem. Physik* 1 (1811):501–505.
   Translated by Gehlen.

   1810:11, 12, and 13 were originally submitted by Davy to
   Gay-Lussac and Thenard for publication in *Ann. chim.*,
   which they edited. They refused to publish them. Davy
   then asked DelaMétherie to publish the papers in *J. phys.
   chim. histoire nat. arts*, appealing to him as a "lover of truth
   and justice." Davy's letter of request is described in that journal (71:43–44) as a note to the translation of Davy's fourth
   Bakerian lecture (see 1809:11T). According to Gerrit Moll,
   Gay-Lussac and Thenard threatened that DelaMétherie's
   journal would be suppressed by the police, were Davy's
   papers published, but the threat proved an idle one—Agassi,
   Isis 52 (1961):88–89. John Davy did not include the papers in
   Works, although he alluded to them in a note, because, he
   said, they contained no new experimental material. (*Works*,
   V, 505.)

C. *Ann. Physik (Halle)* 36:204–243.
   Gilbert translated, cut and rearranged the three papers
   to accommodate translations of Gay-Lussac and Thenard's replies.

Jahrb. Chem. Physik 3 (1811):334–352.
Schweigger's pastiche from the experimental proofs
Davy offered against claims made by Gay-Lussac, Then-
ard, Curaudau, and Ritter.

14.★ Researches on the oxymuriatic acid, its nature and combinations; and on the elements of the muriatic acid. With
some experiments on sulphur and phosphorus, made in
the laboratory of the Royal Institution

Phil. Trans. [100]:231–257.
Issued separately, W. Bulmer, 29 pp.
Royal Society manuscript PT. 4.14.
Read to the Royal Society on 12 July.

R. *Phil. Mag.* 36:352–361, 404–413.
J. Nat Phil. Chem Arts 27:321–337; 28 (1811):31–37.
The elementary nature of chlorine . . . 1809–1818. Edinburgh:
William F. Clay; London: Simpkin, Marshall, Hamilton,
Kent, 1894, pp. 21–39 (Alembic club reprint, no. 9).
Reprint of Davy's pp. 231–250.
A. *J. Nat. Phil. Chem. Arts* 27:78.
Phil. Mag 36:70–71; 152–153.
The first abstract was inaccurate. Pages 152–153 correct
it and list Davy's conclusions.
Monthly Rev. 64 (1811):227–228.
Reviewed by John Bostock.
Monthly Mag. 30:265.
Edin. Rev. 17 (1810–11):402–409.
Reviewed by Henry Brougham.
T. *J. phys. chim. histoire nat. arts* 71:326–348.
A note at the end of the translation quotes a letter from
Davy to Pictet. DelaMétherie's editorial comments on
the substance of the paper appear on pp. 451–454.
Ann. chim. 76:112–128, 129–158.
Translated by Anatole Riffault.
Jahrb. Chem. Physik 3 (1811):95–120.
Gehlen's retranslation of Riffault, collated with 1810:14C,
Bibl. brit., below. Both Gehlen and Schweigger added
notes.
Ann. Physik (Halle) 39 (1811):1–42.
Translated by Gilbert from a collation of three French
versions.
C. *Bibl. brit.* 45:229–262.
J. phys. chim. histoire nat. arts 71:76.

Abstract of a letter from London, dated 18 July, describing some of Davy's experiments.
Ann. Physik (Halle) 36:281–284.
Gilbert's preliminaty report.
Bull. sci. soc. philomathique ns 2 (1810):128–129.
Extracted from a letter dated London, 18 July.

{15.*} [Extract from a lecture on oxymuriatic acid]
Works, VIII, 311–319.

16.* The Bakerian lecture. On some of the combinations of oxy-muriatic gas and oxygene, and on the chemical relations of these principles, to inflammable bodies

Phil. Trans. [101] (1811):1–35.
Issued separately, London: W. Bulmer, 1811, 35 pp.
Royal Society manuscript PT. 5.1.
Davy's fifth Bakerian lecture, read to the Royal Society 15 November. Davy's corrections for the paper appear in a note to 1811:3, p. 162.

R. *Phil. Mag.* 37 (1811):401–423.
Corrections to the reprint are in 38 (1811):18n.
J. Nat. Phil. Chem. Arts 29 (1811):112–127, 222–236.
The elementary nature of chlorine . . . 1809–1818, Edinburgh: William F. Clay; London: Simpkin, Marshall, Hamilton, Kent, 1894, pp. 40–62 (Alembic club reprint, no. 9).
Reprint of Davy's pp. 1–3, 12–35.

A. *Phil. Mag.* 36:392–394, 469–470.
Edin. Rev. 18 (1811):470–480.
Reviewed by Henry Brougham [?].
Monthly Rev. 67 (1812):254–255.
Reviewed by John Bostock.

T. *J. phys. chim. histoire nat. arts* 72 (1811): 358–386.
Ann. chim. 78 (1811):298–333; 79 (1811):5–35.
Translated by Prieur. Quarreling with Davy's nomenclature, Prieur set the terms he preferred (for example, "murigene" for "acide muriatique oxigene") in parentheses within the text.
Ann. Physik (Halle) 39 (1811):43–89.
Translated by Gilbert from *Phil. Trans.* which Davy had sent to him.
Jahrb. Chem. Physik 3 (1811):205–248.
Translated by R. L. Ruhland from a reprint Davy sent to Gehlen. Schweigger's notes to the translation and comments on Davy's nomenclature appear on pp. 249–255.

c. *Bibl. brit.* 47 (1811):34–52, 245–270, 340–362.

De la Rive's commentary with extended portions of direct translation. De la Rive added notes. In the first section (pp. 34–52) the added notes, signed "D." and written by De la Rive, are 1, p. 37; 1, p. 42; and 2, p. 42. The remainder of the notes, also signed "D.," are translations from the original text. In the second section (pp. 245–270) De la Rive added note 1, p. 245. The unmarked note on p. 247 is a translation from the original. De la Rive wrote note 1 on p. 254. He placed parenthetically in the text Davy's original note that appeared on p. 14 of *Phil. Trans.* De la Rive also added note 1, p. 258. In the third section (pp. 340–362) he expanded Davy's asterisk-marked note "From chloros" into a long discussion on nomenclature, which he labeled "note 1" (p. 356).

Bull. sci. soc. philomathique ns 2 (1811):344–346.

Thenard's abstract of the first portion of Prieur's translation in *Ann. chim.*

Bull. sci. soc. philomathique ns 2 (1811):351–355.

Ampère's abstract of De la Rive's commentary, in *Bibl. brit.*

1811

1.* On the nature of bogs in general

Parl. pap., vol. VI (*Reports of Commissioners*), no. 96, 1810–1811, "The second report of the commissioners appointed to enquire into the nature and extent of the several bogs in Ireland, and the practicability of draining and cultivating them, appendix no. 9. Copy of a letter from Mr. Davy, to the Secretary of the Commissioners," pp. 205–206.

Davy's letter, addressed to B. H. Macarthy, Esq., was dated 1 February.

2. [Letter to André-Marie Ampère]

Ann. chim., s. 2, 1 (1816):21–22.

Davy's letter, dated 8 February, complimented Ampère on his masterful discussion of the analogies between fluoric and muriatic gas; Davy, however, found that when potassium burned in silicated fluoric gas, potash was produced, pointing to the existence of some oxygen in the gas. (See 1813:1.)

R. *Correspondance du Grand Ampère*, L. De Launay, editor, Paris, 1936, I, 363.

3.★ On a combination of oxymuriatic gas and oxygene gas

Phil. Trans. [101]: 155–162.
Issued separately, London: W. Bulmer, 8 pp.
Royal Society manuscript PT. 5.8.
   Read to the Royal Society 21 February. Davy's final note
   (p. 162) corrected errors in 1810:16.

R. *Phil. Mag.* 38:13–18.
J. Nat. Phil. Chem. Arts 29:268–274.
The elementary nature of chlorine . . . 1809–1818, Edinburgh:
William F. Clay; London: Simpkin, Marshall, Hamilton,
Kent, 1894, pp. 63–70 (Alembic club reprint, no. 9).
A. *Phil. Mag.* 37:153.
Edin. Rev. 18:470–480.
   Reviewed by Henry Brougham [?].
T. *Bibl. brit.* 47:146–158.
   Translated by De la Rive from a manuscript Davy
   supplied.
J. phys. chim. histoire nat. arts 73:81–88.
   Reprint of De la Rive's translation.
Ann. chim. 79:316–329.
   Davy corrected and emended De la Rive's translation in a
   letter to Berthollet. This reprinting included all of Davy's
   suggested changes.
Ann. Physik (Halle) 39:90–100.
   Translated by Gilbert from *Bibl. brit.*, above.
Jahrb. Chem. Physik 3:256–267.
   Translation based on the corrected and emended French
   translation in *Ann. chim.*, above.
C. *Ann. chim.* 78:93–94.

{4.★} Introductory geological lecture

Works, VIII, 180–200.
   Davy's first lecture of the 1811 course, which was based
   on his series of 1805. See 1805:{5}.

{5.★} Geology—Lecture II

Works, VIII, 201–222.

{6.★} [On the phenomena and causes of volcanoes]

Works, VIII, 223–238.
   Extract from Davy's sixth lecture in the geology course.

7. *Sketch of Mr. Davy's lectures on geology. Delivered at the Royal Institution, London, 1811. From notes taken by a private gentleman* [Thomas Allan]

> Allan attended Davy's lectures so that he could report them to his newspaper, *Caledonian Mercury*. Davy complained that Allan made him too much a Neptunist; Davy thought he actually leaned the other way. Copies exist in the British Museum and the John Crerar Library.

A. *Phil. Mag.* 37:392–398, 465–470.

8. [Letter to Professor Gilbert]

T. *Ann. Physik (Halle)* 38:464–466.
> Davy concurred with Gilbert's opinion on the inaccuracy of the French translation of his papers and letters, but said he had great respect for those published by Pictet. He further stated that he did not now think that nitrogen could be decomposed, and that Scheele's gas [chlorine] contains no oxygen.

{9.*} [The natural advantages of Ireland]

> *Works*, VII, 165.
> Extract from Davy's Dublin lecture series.

{10.*} [On the fitness of modern times for the cultivation of science]

> *Works*, VIII, 319–321.
> Extract from a lecture series.

{11.*} [On the general doctrines of alchemy]

> *Works*, VIII, 328–334.
> Extract from a lecture series.

{12.*} [On the phlogiston theory]

> *Works*, VIII, 337–344.
> Extract from a lecture series.

{13.*} [On the value to women of knowing mathematics]

> *Works*, VIII, 353–355.

1812

{1.⋆} [On the active powers of nature]

> *Works*, VIII, 334–337.
> Extract from a lecture series.

{2.⋆} [On the unknown in science]

> *Works*, VIII, 351.

3.   [Elements of chemical philosophy,—a lecture series at the Royal Institution]

> A. *Monthly Mag.* 33:159–160, 259–263.
> Report of Davy's lectures delivered on 25 January, 1, 8, 15, and 22 February, with descriptions of Davy's demonstration experiments.
> *Phil. Mag.* 39:74–77, 132–140.

4.⋆ On some combinations of phosphorus and sulphur, and on some other subjects of chemical inquiry

> *Phil. Trans.* [102]:405–415.
> Royal Society manuscript PT. 6. 21.
> Read to the Royal Society 18 June.

> R. *Phil. Mag.* 40:417–424.
> *J. Nat. Phil. Chem. Arts* 33:354–362.
> A. *Phil. Mag.* 39:459; 40:152.
> *Ann. Phil.* 1 (1813):215–216.
> *Monthly Rev.* 72 (1813):54.
> Reviewed by John Bostock.
> T. *Bibl. brit.* 52 (1813):232–247.
> *Jahrb. Chem. Physik* 7 (1813):494–516.
> Schweigger's retranslation from *Bibl. brit.*, above. The copious notes he added related to applications of Dalton's theory of definite proportions.
> *Ann. Physik (Halle)* 46 (1814):273–287.
> Translated by Gilbert; his added notes are to explain Davy's system of assigning numbers to the elements.
> *J. phys. chim. histoire nat. arts* 77 (1813):77–85.

5.⋆ On a new detonating compound, in a letter from Sir H. Davy, L.L.D., F.R.S., to the right honourable Sir Joseph Banks, Bart. K.B., P.R.S.

Phil. Trans. [103] (1813):1–7.
Royal Society manuscript PT. 7. 1.
Read to the Royal Society 5 November. See also 1813:3.

R. *Phil. Mag.* 42 (1813):190–193.
A. *Phil. Mag.* 40:387.
   J. Nat. Phil. Chem. Arts 33:320.
   Ann. Phil. 1 (1813):63–64, 71; 2 (1813):227.
   Monthly Rev. 74 (1814):69–70.
   Reviewed by John Bostock.
T. *J. phys. chim. histoire nat. arts* 77 (1813):53–57.
C. *Bibl. brit.* 51:390–392.
   A. Marcet was with Davy when he first prepared nitrogen trichloride, and wrote to Prevost to describe the procedure and to report Davy's accident.
   Bibl. brit. 52 (1813):294–296.
   Marcet's letter of 5 December to Pictet describing Davy's accident and the preparative procedure for NCl_3.
   Ann. Physik (Halle) 47 (1814):49–55.

6.⋆ Elements of chemical philosophy . . . . Part 1, volume 1

J. Johnson and Company, London. xiv, 1 l., 511, 1 l. pl. x. 23 cm. No subsequent volumes were published.
   Davy dedicated the volume to his wife. The manuscript of the dedication is in the collection of John Fulton in the History of Medicine Library of Yale University.

R. *Elements of chemical philosophy.* By Sir Humphry Davy. pt. 1, v. 1, Philadelphia and New York: Bradsford and Inskeep. xii, 296 pp. x [12] pl. 22 cm.
   The plates are numbered I, II, IV, IV, V, V, VII, VIII, IX, X.
A. *Phil. Mag.* 40:145–151, 297–307, 434–444.
   Ann. Phil. 1 (1813):371–377.
   Quart. Rev. 8:65–86.
   Monthly Rev. 72 (1813):148–158.
   Reviewed by John Bostock.
   Phil. Mag. 46 (1815):231–232, 313–316, 397–398.
   Discussions of the many additions made by Van Mons (see below) in his translation of Davy's work.
T. *Eléments des philosophie chimique, par M. le chevalier Homfrede Davy* . . . Traduit de l'anglais, par J. B. Van Mons, Paris and Amsterdam: J.-E.-G.-Du Four, 1813. 2 vols.
   Cited in Bolton (not seen).
   Another edition. 1813–1816, 2 vol. in 8°, without the plates.
   Cited in Quérard (not seen).

J. phys. chim. histoire nat. arts 78 (1814):229–233.

A critique of Van Mons translation.

Eléments de philosophie chimique traduit de l'anglais avec des additions par J. B. van Mons. 1826.

Another edition cited in Bolton (not seen).

Eléments de philosophie chimique, traduit de l'anglais avec des additions par Van Mons. Paris, 1829, 2 vols.

Another edition cited in Quérard (not seen).

Elemente des chemischen Theils der Naturwissenschaft, aus dem englischen übersetzt von Friedrich Wolff. Part 1, volume 1. Berlin: Voss, 1814.

Cited in Bolton (not seen).

Beitrage zur Eweiterung des chemischen Theils der Naturlehre. Translated by F. Wolff. Berlin: Voss, 1820.

Another edition, cited in Kayser (not seen).

Elementi di filosofia chimica . . . Tradotti dall'Inglese in Francese dal sig. G. B. Van-Mons e in Italiana dal sig. dott. G. Con note de sigg. Prof. L. V. Brugnatelli e P. Configliachi. Vol I. Milano, 1814.

Cited by Edinburgh (not seen).

Elementi di filosofia chimica, tradotti e commentati da G. Moretti e G. Prims. Milano, 1814, 2 vols, pls.

Cited in Bolton (not seen).

Elementi di filosofia chimica. Napoli, 1816, 3 vols,. illus.

Cited in Bolton (not seen).

c. *Bibl. brit.* 53 (1813):117–144, 213–234; 55 (1814):183–212, 286–307; 56 (1814):39–56; 57 (1814):47–66.

Jahrb. Chem. Physik 8 (1813):333–343.

Translation by Schweigger of the first two excerpts in *Bibl. brit.*, above, with added criticisms.

J. phys. chim. histoire nat. arts 77 (1813):400–414; 78 (1814): 78–100, 105–110, 224, 383–385, 419–441.

Davy's protests to some of DelaMétherie's assertions are reflected in 77:473–474.

1813

1. [Letter to André-Marie Ampère]

    Ann. chim., s. 2, 2 (1816):22–24.

    Davy's letter of 6 March reverses the opinion he expressed in 1811:2; he now believes that potash is not formed when potassium is burned in silicated fluoric gas.

R. *Correspondance du Grand Ampère*, L. De Launay, ed. Paris, 1936–1943, II, 430–431.

2. On the cause of the changes of colour produced by heat on the surfaces of steel

   Ann. Phil. 1:131–132.

A. *Ann. Phil.* 3 (1814):17.
T. *Jahrb. Chem. Physik* 11 (1814):47–49.
   Schweigger's added notes to his translation are collected on pp. 49–50. Schweigger called for recognition of J. W. von Goethe's theory of light and of the early work of Stoddart.
   Ann. Physik (Halle) 51 (1815):206–208.
   Translated by Gilbert.
   Bibl. brit. 55 (1814):157–160.

3.* Some further observations on a new detonating substance. In a letter from Sir Humphry Davy, L.L.D., F.R.S., V.P.R.S., to the Right Hon. Sir Joseph Banks, Bart., K.B., P.R.S.

   Phil. Trans. [103]:242–251.
   Royal Society manuscript PT. 7. 28.
   Read to the Royal Society on 1 July. See also 1812:5.

R. *Phil. Mag.* 42:321–327.
A. *Ann. Phil.* 2:150–151, 227; 3 (1814):382–383.
   Phil. Mag. 42 (1813):72–73.
   Monthly Rev. 74 (1814):161–162.
   Reviewed by John Bostock.
T. *J. phys. chim. histoire nat. arts* 77:448–455.
   Ann. chim. 89 (1814):5–19.
C. *Bibl. brit.* 54:164–165.
   Jahrb. Chem. Physik 9:208–209.
   Ann. Physik (Halle) 47 (1814):49–55.

4.* Some experiments and observations on the substances produced in different chemical processes on fluor spar

   Phil. Trans. [103]:263–279.
   Royal Society manuscript PT. 7. 31.
   Read to the Royal Society 8 July.

R. *Phil. Mag.* 42:407–418.
A. *Phil. Mag.* 42:72–73.
   Ann. Phil. 3 (1814):382–383.
   Ostensibly reported by Thomas Thomson, the editor of

the journal. He claimed that the printed paper differed markedly from what Davy read to the Royal Society.

T. *J. phys. chim. histoire nat. arts* 77:387–399.
   Davy's corrections to this translation are on p. 474.
   Ann. chim. 88:271–297.
C. *Jahrb. Chem. Physik* 9:210–221.

5. Sur la nouvelle substance [iode] découverte par M. Courtois

T. *Ann. chim.* 88:322–329.
   Davy's letter to Baron Cuvier dated Paris, 11 December, was read to the Institute on 13 December.
   J. phys. chim. histoire nat. arts 77:456–460.
   Giorn. fis. chim. storia nat. 7 (1814):105–109.
   Ann. Physik (Halle) 48 (1814):32–39.
   Translated by Gilbert.

6. Elements of agricultural chemistry, in a course of lectures for the Board of Agriculture

   London: Longman, Hurst, Rees, Orme and Brown; Edinburgh: A. Constable. Pp. viii. 323 lxii [4] p. plates (part fold) 28 × 22 cm. Appendix: An Account of the results of experiments on the produce and nutritive qualities of different grasses and other plants, used as the food of animals. Instituted by John, Duke of Bedford (lxiii pp.), by George Sinclair, edited by Sir H. Davy.

R. *Elements of agricultural chemistry, in a course of lectures for the Board of agriculture.* By Sir Humphry Davy . . . . Philadelphia: John Conrad; Baltimore: Fielding Lucas, Jr.; Alexandria: Robert Gray; and Fredricksburgh [Va.]: William F. Gray. 1815.
   Another edition. *Elements of Agricultural Chemistry, etc. To which is added A Treatise of Soils and Manures, as founded on actual principles of agriculture; in which the theory and doctrines of Sir Humphry Davy, and other agricultural chemists, are rendered familiar to the experienced farmer.* By a practical agriculturist. Philadelphia: B. Warner; Baltimore: Fielding Lucas, Jr. etc. 304, 92 p. illus. 23 cm. "Appendix. An Account of the results of experiments [by George Sinclair] on the produce and nutritive qualities of different grasses and other plants used as the food of animals. Instituted by John Duke of Bedford." pp.[253]–304.
   Davy wrote "Introduction by the Editor," pp. iii–iv of the Appendix, as well as the "Observations on the

chemical composition of the nutritive matter afforded by the grasses in their different states. By the editor." pp. lxi–lxiii.

Another edition. Eastburn, Kirk and Company: New York; Ward and Lily: Boston. 1815, 332 pp.
    Cited in AB (not seen).

"Second American edition." Hudson and Company: Hartford, 1819, 304 pp.
    Cited in AB (not seen).

T. *Elemente de Agricultur-Chemie. Vorlesen gehalten vor den Ackerbaugesellschaft; aus den Englisch von F. Wolff, mit Anmerkungen von A. G. Thaer.* Berlin: Nicolai, 1814.
    Cited in Heinsius (not seen).

Chemisch-Agron. Untersuchungen über den Werth verschiedener Füttergradier. Herausgegeben von H. Davy. Aus den Englisch von U. U. Haas. Trier, 1821.
    Cited in Heinsius (not seen).

Elemente di chimica agraria, tradotti da A. Targione-Tozzetti. 2 vols. Florence, 1815.
    Cited in Bolton (not seen).

Eléments de chimie agricole en un cours de leçons . . . par Sir Humphry Davy . . . Traduit de l'anglais, avec un traité sur l'art de faire le vin et de distiller les eaux-de-vie, par A. Bulos. Paris: Ladrange, 1819, 2 vols.
    Cited in BN (not seen).

Eléments de chimie appliqués à l'agriculture suivis d'un traité sur la chimie des terres, traduit littéral de l'anglais par Marchais de Migneaux. Paris: Crevot, 1820, 1 vol., 6 pl.
    Another translation, cited in Quérard (not seen).

*L'Art de préparer les terres et d'appliquer les engrais, ou chimie appliquée à l'agriculture, par Sir Humphry Davy . . . Tra-*duit de l'anglais, par A. Bulos. Paris: Baudouin, 1825, 499 pp.
    Cited in BN (not seen).

7.   Elements of agricultural chemistry, in a course of lectures for the Board of Agriculture. Longman, Hurst, Rees, Orme, and Brown: London. A. Constable and Co.: Edinburgh. 1814. xi, 479 pp. 8°.

    The second edition, cited in BM (not seen).

R. Reprinted in 8°, 1814, 1823*, and 1827.
    Cited in BM (not seen).

A. *Quart. Rev.* 2:318–331.
    Edin. Rev. 22 (1813–1814):251–281.

On the science of agriculture; comprising a commentary on . . .
the agricultural chemistry of Mr. Kirwan and Sir Humphry
Davy, etc. [With special reference to the "Elements of
agricultural chemistry."] London, 1825.
   Cited in BM (not seen).

c. Traduction libre et abrégée des leçons de chimie, données par le
   chevalier Humphrey [sic] Davy, à la Société d'agriculture de
   Londres, ed. de 1814 . . . Montreal: J. Lane, 1820. 1 p., l., [v]–
   viii pp. 1 l., [9]–123 pp. 22 cm.
   Translated by Anthony Gilbert Douglas.

8. Elements of agricultural chemistry, in a course of lectures
    for the Board of Agriculture, delivered between 1802 and
    1812.

    London: Longman, Hurst, Rees, Orme, and Brown; Edin-
    burgh: A. Constable and Co., 1821. 2 l., x pp., [3]–415 pp.,
    pls. (all folded). 23.5 × 15 cm.
       The third edition. The "Appendix" (pp. 343–400) is
    augmented by "Notes," by Thomas Andrew Knight (pp.
    401–407). Davy supplied a paragraph of introduction
    (p. 401) and, in addition, a final section to the notes (p.
    407) on how Berard of Montpelier reported that the
    ripening of fruit may be delayed by storage in an oxygen-
    poor atmosphere. Pages 409–412 contain the index to the
    volume; pp. 413–415 index the appendix. (Copy in the
    library of J. Z. Fullmer.)

9.* Elements of agricultural chemistry, in a course of lectures
    for the Board of Agriculture, 1802–1812

    R. Works, VII, pp. 169–391; VIII, pp. [v]–148.
        The last edition to be corrected by Davy. (See 1813:7R.)
        The "Appendix" is augmented in the following ways:
        "Of the time in which different grasses produce flowers
        and seeds," a long table with some prefatory matter (pp.
        141–143); a short section, "Of the different soils referred
        to in the appendix" (p. 144); "Observations on the
        chemical composition of the nutritive matter afforded
        by the grasses in their states" (pp. 144–148). John Davy
        has also added Davy's letter to B. H. Macarthy on the bogs
        of Ireland (see 1811:1) as Appendix II (pp. 148–152).
    R. The fifth edition. London: Longman, Rees, Orme, Brown,
        Green, and Longman, 1836. viii, 413 pp.
        The edition has notes by John Davy, and is without the
        "Treatise on soils and manures." Cited by BM (not seen).

The sixth edition. London: Longman, 1839. xii, 422 pp.
Cited by BN (not seen).

[Another edition, without the appendix.] *A new edition, with instructions for the analysis of soils, and copious notes, embracing the recent discoveries in agricultural chemistry.* By John Shier. Glasgow: Richard Griffin; London: Thomas Tegg, 1844. [v]–ix, [1], 293, [1], illus.

The copy in the Library of Congress wants a title page. *A new edition. With instructions for the analysis of soils and copious notes embracing the recent discoveries in agricultural chemistry, by Liebig, Boussingault and others.* By John Shier. London, 1846. ix, 293 pp.
Cited by Bolton (not seen).

[Another edition.] By John Shier. London: Griffin, 1855.
Cited by ECB (not seen).

A. *Chymistry applied to agriculture . . . With a preliminary chapter on the organization, structure, etc. of plants by Sir Humphry Davy, and an essay on the use of lime as a manure, by M. Pervis, with introductory observations to the same by James Renwick . . .* Translated [from J. A. C. Chaptal, Count de Chanteloup, Chimie apliquée à l'agriculture.] and edited by Rev. W. P. Page. New York: Harper and Brothers, 1840. 359 pp., 12°

The section taken from Davy appears on pp. 25–76.
Cited in BM (not seen).

T. *Nouveau manuel de chimie agricole, traduit sur cinquième edition anglaise de Eléments de chimie agricole de Sir Humphry Davy, avec les notes de M. John Davy sur des faits connus seulement depuis 1826.* A. D. Vergnaud. Paris: [Encyclopédie-Roret], 1838. vi, 305 pp., pl. 5, 18°.

Cited in BM (not seen).
Osnovaniia zemledel'cheskoi khimii izlozhennyia serom Gemfri Devi. St. Petersburg, 1832. 8°
Cited in Bolton (not seen).

1814

1.⋆ Some experiments and observations on a new substance which becomes a violet coloured gas by heat

Phil. Trans. [104]:74–93.
Royal Society manuscript PT. 8.6.
Read to the Royal Society on 20 January.

R. *Phil. Mag.* 44:3–15.
A. *Edin. Rev.* 23:486–493.
   Reviewed by Henry Brougham.
   Phil. Mag. 43:69–70.
   Ann. Phil. 3:73–74, 146–148; 4:441–444.
   Monthly Rev. 75:413–415.
   Reviewed by John Bostock.
T. *Bibl. brit.* 56:248–275.
   De la Rive's translation.
   Ann. chim. 92:89–116.
   De la Rive's translation.
   J. phys. chim. histoire nat. arts 79:153–167.
   Davy sent a corrected copy of De la Rive's translation to DelaMétherie, who reprinted the paper incorporating Davy's corrections. Davy's letter of transmission, translated, appears as a note.
C. *Jahrb. Chem. Physik* 11:68–73.
   Schweigger, who based his translation on the abstract published in *Ann. Phil.*, above, introduced his objections to the nomenclature Davy used on pp. 73–75.
   Ann. Physik (Halle) 48:19–22.
   Translated by Gilbert from the abstract in *Phil. Mag.*, above.

2.* An account of some new experiments on the fluoric compounds; with some observations on other objects of chemical inquiry

   Phil. Trans. [104]:62–73.
   Royal Society manuscript PT. 8.5.
   Read to the Royal Society 13 February.

R. *Phil. Mag.* 44:93–100.
   The elementary nature of chlorine . . . 1809–1818, Edinburgh: William F. Clay; London: Simpkin, Marshall, Hamilton, Kent, 1894, pp. 71–75 (Alembic club reprint, no. 9).
A. *Phil. Mag.* 43:154.
   Ann. Phil. 3:226–229; 4:441–444.
   Monthly Mag. 37:451–452.
   Monthly Rev. 75:412–413.
   Reviewed by John Bostock.
T. *Bibl. brit.* 56:354–370.
   Translated by De la Rive.
C. *J. phys. chim. histoire nat. arts* 79:259–267.
   Bibl. brit. 56:296–299.
   Ann. Physik (Halle) 46:288–293.

Davy's results were reported to Gilbert in a letter from Van Mons in Brussels.

3.* Further experiments and observations on iodine

Phil. Trans. [104]:487–507.
Royal Society manuscript PT. 8.25.
Read to the Royal Society 16 June.

R. *Phil. Mag.* 44:355–368.
A. *Ann. Phil.* 6 (1815):136–138.
Monthly Rev. 76 (1815):40–42.
Reviewed by John Bostock.
T. *Bibl. brit.* 57:243–258, 335–351.
Translated by De la Rive.
C. *Jahrb. Chem. Physik* 12:234–237.

4.* Some experiments on the combustion of the diamond and other carbonaceous substances

Phil. Trans. [104]:557–570.
Royal Society manuscript PT. 8.28.
Read to the Royal Society 23 June.

R. *Phil. Mag.* 44:429–438.
A. *Phil. Mag.* 43:457.
Ann. Phil. 6 (1815):139.
Quart. J. Sci. 4 (1817):155.
Monthly Rev. 76 (1815):45–46.
Reviewed by John Bostock.
T. *Ann. chim.*, s. 2, 1 (1816):16–31.
Bibl. brit. 57:126–146.
Translated by De la Rive.
J. phys. chim. histoire nat. arts 85 (1817):398–399.
Jahrb. Chem. Phys. 12:200–216.
Schweigger added notes to his translation.
Ann. Physik (Halle) 50 (1815):1–20
Translated by Gilbert.
C. *Bull. sci. soc. philomathique* 1815, pp. 42–43; 1817, pp. 174–175.
The first of these two extracts was made by M. E. Chevreul from De la Rive's translation. The second was derived from the abstract in *Quart. J. Sci.*

1815

1. [Letter to De la Rive]
T. *Bibl. brit.* 58:190–191.

Davy's letter dated Rome, 6 February 1815, reported his work on the colors used by the ancients (see 1815:2) and a new solid compound of iodine and oxygen (see 1815:4).
Ann. Physik (Halle) 51:336–337.

2.★ Some experiments and observations on the colours used in painting by the ancients

Phil. Trans. [105]:97–124.
Royal Society manuscript PT. 9.8.
Read to the Royal Society 23 February.

R. *Phil. Mag.* 45:349–359, 414–422.
A. *Ann. Phil.* 5:307–308; 6:222.
Monthly Mag. 40:427–431.
Monthly Rev. 77:426–428.
Phil. Mag. 45:151, 220.
Quart. Rev. 14 (1815–1816):407.
T. *Bibl. brit.* 59:226–238, 336–346; 60:129–148.
Ann. chim. 96:72–95, 193–212.
Ann. Physik (Halle) 52 (1816):1–55.
Translated by Gilbert, who added notes to correlate Davy's comments on pigments with a text of Pliny's.
C. See 1815:1.
Bibl. brit. 60:281–282.

3. [Report of a letter describing a jet of natural gas near Pietra Mala]

A. *Ann. Phil.* 5:233–235.
A. B. Granville's corrections to Thomson's previous report (*Ann. Phil.* 5:74) are based directly on Davy's letter. Thomson's report was based on his memory of the letter.
T. *Bibl. brit.* 58:369–373.
Ann. Physik (Halle) 52 (1816):345–348.
Gilbert's translation also called attention to Volta's work on the same subject.

4.★ Some experiments on a solid compound of iodine and oxygene, and on its chemical agencies

Phil. Trans. [105]:203–213.
Royal Society manuscript PT. 9.12.
Read to the Royal Society 20 April.

R. *Phil. Mag.* 46:345–351.
A. *Phil. Mag.* 45:304.
   Ann. Phil. 5:388–389; 7 (1816):30, 131.
   Monthly Rev. 80 (1816):66–67.
T. *Jahrb. Chem. Physik* 16 (1816):343–351.
   Translated by J. L. G. Meinecke; J. W. Dobereiner contributed a note.
   Ann. chim. 96:289–305.
   Translated by Despretz, who complained of his difficulties in rendering Davy's nomenclature.
C. See 1815:1.
   Bibl. brit. 60:284–285.
   Jahrb. Chem. Physik 13:112–113.
   Thomas Thomson reported Davy's paper to Schweigger on 23 April.

5.* On the action of acids on the salts usually called hyperoxymuriates, and on the gases produced from them

   Phil. Trans. [105]:214–219.
   Royal Society manuscript PT. 9.13.
   Read to the Royal Society 4 May.

R. *Phil. Mag.* 46:426–429.
A. *Ann. Phil.* 5:453–454; 7 (1816):28–31, 131.
   Monthly Mag. 40:167.
   Phil. Mag. 45:375
   Monthly Rev. 80 (1816):67–68.
T. *Ann. chim.*, s. 2, 1 (1816):76–82.
   Translated by Despretz.
C. *Bibl. brit.* 60:285–286.
   J. phys. chim. histoire nat. arts 82 (1816):202–206.

6.* On the fire-damp of coal-mines, and on methods of lighting the mines so as to prevent its explosion

   Phil. Mag. 46:444–458.
   Issued separately, London: Longman and Hunter, 39 pp. + pl.
   Royal Society manuscript PT. 10.1.
   Read to the Royal Society 9 November. The Council released the paper on 25 January 1816 for publication before the appearance of *Phil. Trans.*

R. *Phil. Trans.* [106] (1816):1–21, 22 + pl.
   [Reissued] with an advertisement; containing an account of an invention for lighting the mines and consuming the

fire-damp without danger to the miner. London: Longman and Hunter, 1816. xvi, 39. (See also 1816:1.)

A. *Phil. Mag.* 46:387.
   Edin. Rev. 26 (1816):233–240.
   Reviewed by John Playfair.
   Ann. Phil. 6:453–454; 9 (1817):462–463.
   Monthly Mag. 40 (1815–1816):532–533.
   Monthly Rev. 81 (1816):388–391.

T. *Ann. chim.*, s. 2, 1 (1816):136–157 + pl.
   Translated by Chaptal.
   Bibl. univ. 1 (1816):149–157 + pl.
   The editors changed the order of Davy's sections, but all of the paper was translated. Davy's final section became the introduction.

7. [On Carter's air-tight glove]

   Phil. Mag. 47 (1816):49–50.
   Henry Carter wrote to Davy on 27 December. Davy sent the letter to the editor, appending a note to call the attention of mine owners to Carter's suggestion that an air-tight glove be developed. Davy thought that safety lamps which had gone out could be relighted without danger of explosion, if the operator wore such gloves.

1816

1.★ An account of an invention for giving light in explosive mixtures of fire-damp in coal mines, by consuming the fire-damp

   Phil. Trans. [106]:23–24.
   Royal Society manuscript PT. 10.2.
   Read to the Royal Society 11 January. (See also 1815:6R)

A. *Phil. Mag.* 47:67–68.
   Ann. Phil. 7:135; 9 (1817):462–463.
   Quart. J. Sci. 1:113.
   Monthly Rev. 81 (1816):388–391.

2.★ Further experiments on the combustion of explosive mixtures confined by wire-gauze, with some observations on flame

   Phil. Trans. [106]:115–119.
   Royal Society manuscript PT. 10.5.
   Read to the Royal Society 25 January.

R. *Phil. Mag.* 48:24–27.
A. *Ann. Phil.* 7:225; 9 (1817):462–463.
   Phil. Mag. 47:67–68.
   Quart. J. Sci. 1:113.
   Monthly Rev. 81:388–391.
   Tyne Mercury, 13 February.
T. *Giorn. fis. chim. storia nat.* 10 (1817):253–258.
   (Not seen.)
   Neues J. Pharm. Aerzte Apoth. Chem. 2 (1813):313–325.
   (Not seen.)

3. On the wire-gauze safe-lamps for preventing explosions
    from fire-damp, and for giving light in explosive atmos-
    pheres in coal mines

    Quart. J. Sci. 1:1–5 + pl.
    Dated Grosvenor-street, 25 February.

T. *Ann. chim.,* s. 2, 1:329–332.
   Ann. Physik (Halle) 56 (1817):112–116, 116–125.
   Davy's comments appear as long notes on pp. 126–132,
   to a translation of a letter from John Buddle to Davy.
C. *Bull. sci. soc. philomathique,* pp. 65–66.
   Abstracted by Baillet.

4.* On aqua-regia, or nitro-muriatique acid

    Quart. J. Sci. 1:67–68.

A. *Phil. Mag.* 47:303–304.
T. *Ann. chim.,* s. 2, 1:327–329.
   Ann. Physik (Halle) 57 (1817):296–301.
   Neues J. Pharm. Aerzte Apoth. Chem. 1 (1817):289–292.
   (Not seen.)

5. A few additional practical observations on the wire-gauze
    safety-lamps for miners. With some evidence of their use

    Phil. Mag. 48:51–59.
    The "evidence of use" was in letters from John Buddle
    and John Peile, which Davy appended.

6.* Observations on the preceding paper

    Quart. J. Sci. 1:262–264.
    Davy's extension of Michael Faraday's "On the analysis

of a native caustic lime of Tuscany" (pp. 261–262). Davy supplied a theory to account for the formation of the lime.

7.★ Notice of some experiments and new views respecting flame

    Quart. J. Sci. 2:124–127.
    Paper dated London, 21 July.

  T. *Ann. chim.*, s. 2, 3:129–134.
    Translated by Billy.
    Ann. Physik (Halle) 56 (1817):141–149.
    Translated by Gilbert.
    Bibl. univ. 3:216–220.
  C. *Bull. sci. soc. philomathique* 1816, pp. 163–164.
    Abstracted by J. B. Biot.

8.★ On the analogies between the undecompounded substances, and on the constitution of acids

    Quart. J. Sci. 1:283–288.
    See 1817:5.

  T. *Ann. Physik (Halle)* 54:372–382.
    Translated by Gilbert.

9.★ On the prussic basis and acid

    Quart. J. Sci. 1:288–289.

  T. *Ann. Physik (Halle)* 54:383–385.
    Translated by Gilbert.

10. Suggestions arising from inspection of wire gauze lamps, in their working state, in mines

    Phil. Mag. 48:197–200.
    Paper dated Newcastle, 9 September.

  A. *Newcastle Courant,* 26 October.
    Letter by the Rev. John Hodgson dated High Haworth, 21 October.
    Newcastle Courant, 1 February (1817).
    Hodgson's restatement of the lamp's advantages.

11. Observations on the preceding letter

    Quart. J. Sci. 1:306–307.
    The "preceding letter," from John Buddle to Davy (pp.

302–305), concerned practical applications of the wire gauze safe lamp.

A. *Newcastle Courant*, 25 January (1817).
Buddle's report from Wallsend Colliery on 13 January.

12. The papers of Sir H. Davy . . . communicated to the Royal Society on the fire-damp of coal mines, and on methods of lighting the mines so as to prevent its explosion. &c. With engravings.

As printed in the Royal Society's Transactions for 1816. Newcastle: Emerson Charnley, 1817. 20 pp.

R. Reprint of 1815:7, 1816:3, 5.
C. *Ann. chim.*, s. 2, 4 (1817):110–111.

1817

1.* Some researches on flame.

Phil. Trans. [107]:45–76.
Royal Society manuscript PT. 11.6.
Read to the Royal Society 16 January

R. *Phil. Mag.* 50:3–26.
A. *Ann. Phil.* 9:151; 10:447–452.
Quart. J. Sci. 3:130–131.
Monthly Rev. 84:260–263.
T. *J. phys. chim. histoire nat. arts* 84:148–166, 216–222.
Bibl. univ. 5:199–213, 308–319.
   The anonymous translator supplied an introduction.
Ann. chim., s. 2, 4:260–287, 337–347.
   Translated by Billy.
Giorn. fis. chim. storia nat. 10:165–183, 245–253.
   (Not seen.)
Ann. Physik (Halle) 56:150–184, 225–241.
   Translated by Gilbert, who appended notes to show Davy's use of Gay-Lussac's gas law to calculate flame temperatures.
C. *Bibl. univ.* 4:149–152.
Bull. sci. soc. philomathique, pp. 50–51.
   Abstracted by Biot.

2.* Some new experiments and observations on the combustion of gaseous mixtures, with an account of a method of preserving a continued light in mixtures of inflammable gases and air without flame

Phil. Trans. [107]:77–85 + pl.
Royal Society manuscript PT. 11.7.
  Read to the Royal Society 23 January.

A. *Ann. Phil.* 9:152; 10:447–452.
  Blackwood's Magazine 2 (1818):699.
  Quart. J. Sci. 5:128.
  Monthly Mag. 47 (1819):265.
  Mirror 3 (1824):216.
  Monthly Rev. 84:263–264.
T. *J. phys. chim. histoire nat. arts* 84:223–228.
  Jahrb. Chem. Physik 20 (1818):175–183.
  Ann. chim., s. 2, 4:347–356; s. 2, 5:315–317.
    Description of the plate diagrams on pp. 315–317.
  Ann. Physik (Halle) 56:242–255, 437–439.
    Translated by Gilbert.
C. *Bibl. univ.* 4:153–157.
    Marcet's letter to Prevost, giving experimental details for the lamp without flame, and a theoretical explanation of how the lamp operates.
  Bibl. univ. 5:81–84, 319–321.
  Ann. chim., s. 2, 7 (1818):207–208; 8 (1818):443.
  Bull. sci. soc. philomathique, p. 65.
    Abstracted by Biot.

3. [Extract of a letter to the Reverend John Hodgson]

Phil. Mag. 50:231–232 + pl.
    Davy's letter explained how a platinum tissue introduced in the top of the common wire-gauze lamp rendered the flame visible.

R. *Lit. Gaz.* 1:398.
A. *Blackwood's Magazine* 2:97.
T. *Bibl. univ.* 6:154, pl., 231–232.
C. *Bull. sci. soc. philomathique* p. 180.

4.★ On the cause of the diminution of the temperature of the sea on approaching land, or in passing over banks in the ocean

Quart. J. Sci. 3:368–370.

T. *Ann. chim.*, s. 2, 5:395–404.
    The long note on p. 401 was added by Gay-Lussac.

Jahrb. Chem. Phys. 21 (1818):361–370.
Long notes added by the translator, plus a translation of Gay-Lussac's note, above.
Ann. Physik (Halle) 66 (1820):139–145.
Translated by Gilbert, who added the tabular data in the notes.

5.★ Remarks on a note in the second number of this journal

Quart. J. Sci. 3:378–379.
Davy's remarks continue his paper, 1816:8, to establish more solidly his priority claim in the iodine controversy, as well as to acknowledge his debts to Gay-Lussac and Baron von Humboldt in eudiometry.

6. Vegetables

The cyclopedia; or, universal dictionary of arts, sciences, and literature, Abraham Rees, ed. London: Longman, Hurst, Rees, Orme, and Brown, 1819, Vol. 36, Tolerium-Vermelho.
Davy is listed by Rees as one of the authors of sections in "Chemistry" in the Introduction (I, v). Rees divided "Chemistry" into several subtopics. Although the date of publication for each of the volumes is given as 1819, the volumes were published in varying years. *Phil. Mag.* 56 (1820):218–224 and B. D. Jackson, *An attempt to ascertain the actual dates of publication of the various parts of Rees's Cyclopaedia,* London: Pewtress, 1895, 5 pp., both give the date of publication for this volume as 24 October 1817. The article in *Phil. Mag.* provides additional confirmation for Davy's authorship.

1818

1.★ On the fallacy of experiments in which water is said to have been formed by the decomposition of chlorine

Phil. Trans. [108]:169–171.
Royal Society manuscript PT. 12.10.
Read to the Royal Society 12 February.

R. *Phil. Mag.* 53 (1819):326–328.
The elementary nature of chlorine . . . 1809–1818, Edinburgh: William F. Clay; London: Simpkin, Marshall, Hamilton, Kent, 1894, pp. 75–77 (Alembic club reprint, no. 9).

A. *Ann. Phil.* 11:220; 12:450.
    Monthly Rev. 87:189.
    Phil. Mag. 51:139.
    Blackwood's Magazine 2:699.
C. *J. phys. chim. histoire nat. arts* 86:245.
    Bibl. univ. 9:77–78.
    Ann. chim., s. 2, 7:217.

2.* New experiments on some of the combinations of phosphorus

    Phil. Trans. [108]:316–337.
    Royal Society manuscript PT. 12.17.
    Read to the Royal Society 9 April.

R. *Phil. Mag.* 52:440–454.
A. *Ann. Phil.* 11:381–382; 13 (1819):210–214.
    Monthly Rev. 90 (1819):64.
T. *Ann. chim.*, s. 2, 10 (1819):207–219.
    Jahrb. Chem. Physik, 30 (1820):294–316.
        Translated by Meinecke, who added notes. His further comments appear on pp. 316–317.
    Neues J. Pharm. Aerzte. Apoth. Chem. 3 (1819):405–421.
    (Not seen.)
C. *J. phys. chim. histoire nat. arts* 88 (1819):65.
    Bibl. univ. 9:80–81.
    Bull. sci. soc. philomathique p. 128.

3.* Hints on the geology of Cornwall

    Trans. Roy. Geol. Soc. Cornwall, 1:38–50.
        Davy's paper was communicated as a letter to Henry Boase, the Treasurer of the society.

4. Instructions for the adjustment and use of the instruments intended for the northern expeditions, printed at the request of the Council of the Royal Society
Use of the electrical apparatus
Use of the apparatus for taking up sea water from given depths
Of the state of the atmosphere in high northern regions

    Quart. J. Sci. 5:227, 227–228, 231–233.
        The entire report appeared on pp. 202–233. The other authors were Captain Henry Kater (pp. 202–223), Sir Henry Englefield (pp. 229–230) and Dr. Wollaston (pp. 223–226).

5.* Some observations on the formation of mists in particular situations

    Phil. Trans. [109] (1819):123–131.
    Royal Society manuscript PT. 13.11.
      Paper, dated Rome, 8 December, was read to the Royal Society 25 February 1819.

  R. *Phil. Mag.* 54 (1819):296–301.
  A. *Ann. Phil.* 13 (1819):305; 15 (1820):50.
    Phil. Mag. 53 (1819):289.
    Edin. Phil. J. 2 (1820):185.
    Monthly Rev. 93 (1820):291–292.
  T. *Ann. chim.,* s. 2, 12 (1819):195–205.
    Giorn. arcad. 5 (1820):44–52.
      (Not seen.)
  C. *Bibl. univ.* 11 (1819):227.
    Bull. sci. soc. philomathique 1819, p. 159.

6. On the safety lamp for coal miners; with some researches on flame

    London: R. Hunter. viii, 148 pp. pl. (part fold) 21.5 cm.

  R. On the safety lamp for preventing explosions in mines, houses lighted by gas, spirit warehouses, or magazines in ships, &c. With some researches on flame. London: R. Hunter, 1825. viii, 152 pp. 1 l. fold front. 22.5 cm.
    A reissue, with additional appendices.
  A. *Phil. Mag.* 51:461.
    The appendices were reprinted.
  T. *Über die Sicherheitslampe zur verhütung von Explosionen in Gruben, gasbeleuchteten Häussern, Spiritlagern oder Schiffsräumern u. dgl. mit einigen Untersuchungen über die Flamme. Abhandlungen von H. Davy, 1815–1817* .... Übersetzt und herausgegeben von Klaus Clusius, etc. Leipzig: Akademische verlagsgesellschaft, 1937. [Ostwald's Klassiker der exakten Wissenschaften ... (nr. 242).] 3 pp. l., 62 pp., 2 fold. pl. 19 cm.

1819

1. Report on the state of the manuscripts of papyrus, found at Herculaneum

    Quart. J. Sci. 7:154–161.
    Davy sent this report, dated Rome, 12 February, to Sir

Joseph Banks. Banks gave it to Dr. Marcet, who sent it to W. T. Brande. Brande published it without Davy's permission, and much to his subsequent annoyance, for Davy regarded it as a private communication. See also 1821:5.

A. *Phil. Mag.* 53:302–304.
   Monthly Mag. 47:355.
   Lit. Gaẓ. 1820, pp. 572–574.
T. *Ann. chim.*, s. 2, 10:414–424.
   Translated by Anatole Riffault.
   Ann. Physik (Halle) 64 (1820):31–44.
   Translated by Gilbert, whose added notes excuse F. K. L. Sickler's failure to unroll the papyri.
C. *J. phys. chim. histoire nat. arts* 88:402–405.

1820

1. [Observations on a stream of lava at Vesuvius]

C. Memoria letta nella seduta de' 17. Marzo 1820 da S. A. reale il principe Cristiano Federico di Danimarca.
   Atti R. Accad. Napoli 2, 2 (1825):[3]–7.
   Davy ascended Vesuvius on 26 January accompanied by the Crown Prince of Denmark and the mineralogist Theodore Monticelli; Prince Christian published his report of their experiments in French.
CT. *Jahrb. Chem. Physik* 34 (1822):447–448.

2.★ On the magnetic phenomena produced by electricity; in a letter from Sir H. Davy, Bart., F.R.S. to W. H. Wollaston, M.D., P.R.S.

   Phil. Trans. [111] (1821):7–19.
   Royal Society manuscript PT. 15.2.
   Read to the Royal Society 16 November.

R. *Phil. Mag.* 58 (1821):43–50.
   Ann. Phil. ns 2 (1821):81–88.
A. *Phil. Mag.* 56:381–382.
   Edin. Phil. J. 4 (1821):167–175.
   Blackwood's Magazine 8:339.
   Monthly Rev. 97 (1822):53–54.
T. *J. phys. chim. histoire nat. arts* 94 (1822):72–81.
   Ann. Physik (Halle) 71 (1822):225–240.

Translated by Gilbert; he added a note to explain his general aims in making translations.

c. *J. phys. chim. histoire nat. arts* 91:394.

3.* [Discourse of the President on assuming the chair of the Royal Society]
> See 1827:1.
> Read to the Royal Society 7 December.

R. Charles Richard Weld, *History of the Royal Society*, vol. II, London: John W. Parker, 1848, pp. 345–355.

A. *Phil. Mag.* 56:450–452.
Quart. J. Sci. 10 (1821):380–386.
Ann. Phil. ns 1 (1821):144–148.
A long abstract to overcome the deficient reporting in ns 1:64–65.

c. *Bibl. univ.* 16 (1821):263–269.
Translated from *Ann. Phil.*, above.

1821

1.* Memoir on a deposit found in the waters at Lucca

Ann. Phil. ns 3 (1822):199–201.
Davy visited Lucca in the summer of 1819. His paper was originally communicated to the Royal Academy of Sciences of Naples [see T. below], which is said to be the source of this English version.

T. Memoria sopra de un deposito trovato ne bagni di lucca.
Atti R. Accad. Napoli, 2. 2 (1825):9–11.
Ann. chim. 19:194–196.
Jahrb. Chem. Physik 35 (1822):78–79.
Translated from *Ann. Phil.*, above.

2. [Letter to John Herapath]

Ann. Phil. ns 2:305.
Davy's letter of 13 January comments on Herapath's kinetic theory.

3. [Letter to André-Marie Ampère]

Bibl. univ. 17:191.
A portion of Davy's letter, dated 10 February, showing the identity of magnetism and electricity was read in translation to the French Academy on 19 March.

A. *Monthly Rev.* 100 (1823):515; 102 (1823):477, 479.
C. *Ann. chim.* 17: 217–218.

4. [Letter to John Herapath]

> *Ann. Phil.* 2:305.
> Davy's letter of 6 March rejects the idea of an absolute zero; Davy sees no connection between heat capacity and temperature.

5.★ Some observations and experiments on the papyri found in the ruins of Herculaneum

> *Phil. Trans.* [111]: 191–208.
> Royal Society manuscript PT. 15.15.
> Read to the Royal Society 15 March. See 1819:1.

R. *Phil. Mag.* 58:421–431.
A. *Quart. J. Sci.* 12 (1822):367–369.
> *Ann. Phil.*, ns 3 (1822):61–63.
> *Monthly Mag.* 53 (1822):57–58.
> *Monthly Rev.* 98 (1822):289–291.

T. *J. phys. chim. histoire nat. arts* 93:401–413.
C. *Bibl. univ.* 17:289–294.
> Abstracted by J. Macaire.
> *Jahrb. Chem. Physik* 34 (1822):259–260.
> Humphry Davy's Versuche, die herkulanensischen Händschriften ... mit Hülfe chem. Mittel zu entwickeln. An Appendix to Friedrich K. L. Sickler's *Die Herculanensischen Händschriften in England und meine ... zu ihrer Entwickelung gemachten Versuche,* Leipzig: Brockhaus, 1819.
> Cited in Heinsius, vol. 6, col. 788 (not seen).

6. Preservation from lightning

A. *Phil. Mag.* 59:468.
> Extracted from Davy's "fourth lecture."

7.★ Farther researches on the magnetic phenomena produced by electricity; with some new experiments on the properties of electrified bodies in their relations to conducting powers and temperatures

> *Phil. Trans.* [111]:425–439.
> Royal Society manuscript PT. 15.31.
> Read to the Royal Society 5 July.

R. *Phil. Mag.* 58:406–415.
   Ann. Phil. ns 3 (1822):1–10.
A. *Quart. J. Sci.* 12 (1822):119, 126, 377–380.
   Monthly Mag. 53 (1822):242.
T. *J. phys. chim. histoire nat. arts* 94 (1822):226–237.
   Ann. Physik (Halle) 71 (1822):241–261.
   Translated by Gilbert.

8.⋆ [The presidential anniversary discourse—I]

   See 1827:1.
   Read to the Royal Society 30 November.

A. *Phil. Mag.* 58:448–449.
   Quart. J. Sci. 12 (1822):300–304.
   Ann. Phil. ns 3 (1822):72–75.

9.⋆ On the electrical phenomena exhibited in vacuo

   Phil. Trans. [112] (1822):64–75.
   Read to the Royal Society 20 December.

R. *Phil. Mag.* 60 (1822):179–186.
A. *Quart. J. Sci.* 14 (1823):165–166.
   Ann. Phil. ns 4 (1822):375–379, 466.
   Edin. Phil. J. 7 (1822):226–230.
   Monthly Mag. 54 (1822):362.
   Monthly Rev. 101 (1823):169–170.
T. *Ann. chim.* 20 (1822):168–182.
   Translated by Billy.
   Ann. Physik (Halle) 72 (1822):357–374.
   Translated by Gilbert.
C. *Jahrb. Chem. Physik* 35 (1822):495–496.

1822

1.⋆ On the state of water and aeriform matter in cavities found
    in certain crystals

   Phil. Trans. [112]:367–376.
   Read to the Royal Society 13 June.

R. *Ann. Phil.* ns 5 (1823):43–49.
A. *Quart. J. Sci.* 14 (1823):385.
   Edin. Phil. J. 7:186–187.
   Monthly Rev. 101 (1823):179.

T. *Ann. chim.* 21:132–143.
C. *Jahrb. Chem. Physik* 36:241; 37 (1823):480.
> The first report was based on the abstract in the *Edin. Phil. J.*; the second, on the translation in *Ann. chim.*, above.

2.⋆ [The presidential anniversary discourse—II]

> See 1827:1.
> Read to the Royal Society 30 November.

A. *Phil. Mag.* 60:459–463.
  Ann. Phil. ns 5 (1823):62–65.

1823

1.⋆ On a new phenomenon of electro-magnetism

> *Phil. Trans.* [113]:153–159.
> Royal Society manuscript PT. 16.14.
> > Read to the Royal Society 6 March.

R. *Ann. Phil.* ns 7 (1824): 22–25.
A. *Quart. J. Sci.* 15:292; 17 (1824):122.
  Ann. Phil. ns 5:303–305.
> > Thomson corrected the report on p. 391.
  Edin. Phil. J. 10 (1824):185–186.
  Monthly Rev. 103 (1824):417–419.
T. *Ann. chim.* 25 (1824):64–71.
> > Translated by Anatole Riffault.
  Jahrb. Chem. Physik 40 (1824):332–350.
> > Translated by L. F. Kaemtz.
C. *Bibl. univ.* 25 (1824):98–103.
  Bull. sci. soc. philomathique 1824, pp. 21–23.

2.⋆ Note on the condensation of muriatic acid gas into the liquid form

> *Phil. Trans.* [113]:164–165.
> Royal Society manuscript PT. 16.16.
> > Read to the Royal Society 13 March. Davy appended this note to Faraday's paper, "On fluid chlorine," pp. 160–164.

R. *Phil. Mag.* 62:415–416.
  Ann. Phil. ns 7 (1824):92–97.

A. *Ann. Phil.* ns 5:303–305.
   Thomson corrected his errors in reporting on p. 391.
   The liquefaction of gases. Papers by Michael Faraday, F.R.S.,
   Edinburgh: William F. Clay; London: Simpkin, Marshall,
   Hamilton, Kent, 1896, pp. 9–10 (Alembic club reprint, no.
   12).
C. *Ann. chim.* 24:401–402.
   Jahrb. Chem. Physik 38:116–122.

3.* On the application of liquids formed by the condensation
   of gases as mechanical agents

   Phil. Trans. [113]:199–203.
   Royal Society manuscript PT. 16.20.
   Read to the Royal Society 17 April.

A. *Ann. Phil.* ns 7 (1824):143–146.
   Quart. J. Sci. 15:292; 17 (1824):125–126.
   Ann. Phil. ns 5:461–462.
   Edin. Phil. J. 10 (1824):191.
   Monthly Rev. 105 (1824):174–175.
T. *Ann. chim.* 25 (1824):80–85.

4.* Appendix to the preceding paper. On the changes of volume
   produced in gases in different states of density, by heat

   Phil. Trans. [113]:204–205.
   Read to the Royal Society 1 May.

A. *Quart. J. Sci.* 15:292.
   Ann. Phil. ns 5:463.
   Phil. Mag. 61:382–383.
   Edin. Phil. J. 10 (1824):192.
   Monthly Rev. 105 (1824): 175–176.
T. *Ann. chim.* 25 (1824):86–87.

5. [Introduction of H. C. Oersted to the Royal Society]

   Davy presided at the Royal Society on 8 May.

A. *Ann. Phil.* ns 5:465.
   Phil. Mag. 61:383.

6. Minutes of evidence. Report from the select committee
   on gas-light establishments

   Parl. pap. vol. V (*Reports from committees,* vol. II), no. 529,
   1823, Report from the select committee on gas-light

establishments, Appendix. Minutes of Evidence. pp. 5–11.
Davy testified on 20 June.

7.⋆ [The presidential anniversary discourse—III]

See 1827:1.
Read to the Royal Society 1 December.

A. *Quart. J. Sci.* 16:298–299.
Lit. Gaz. p. 777.
Phil. Mag. 62:452–454.
Ann. Phil. ns 7 (1824):69.
Thomson wrote the précis from memory, and therefore
thought it might not be completely error-free.

1824

1.⋆ On the corrosion of copper sheeting by sea water, and on
methods of preventing this effect; and on their application
to ships of war and other ships

Phil. Trans. [114]:151–158.
Read to the Royal Society 22 January.

R. *Phil. Mag.* 64:30–35.
Ann. Phil. ns 8:94–98.
A. *Edin. Phil. J.* 10:369–370.
Phil. Mag. 63:60.
Quart. J. Sci. 17:253–254.
Ann. Phil. ns 7:229–230.
Monthly Rev. 106 (1825):74–75.
T. *Ann. chim.* 26:84–92.
C. *Bibl. univ.* 30 (1825):526–527.
Jahrb. Chem. Physik 41:464–465.
Schweigger added notes (pp. 490–492) to this report, based
on that in *Ann. Phil.* 7:229–230, above, to show where
Davy and Ritter differed.
Bull. sci. soc. philomathique p. 16.
Anonymous translation of the report in *Phil. Mag.*, above.
Ann. Physik Chem. 3 (1825):211n.

2. On the salmon fisheries. Appendix no. 3 to the report from
the select committee on salmon fisheries of the United
Kingdom

Parl. pap. vol. VII (*Report from committees,* vol. IV), no. 427, pp. 144–145.
Davy's letter dated 8 May.

A. *Trans. Roy. Soc. Edin.* 12 (1834):498–500.
Critique by Robert Knox.

3.⋆ Additional experiments and observations on the application of electrical combinations to the preservation of the copper sheathing of ships, and to other purposes

Phil. Trans. [114]:243–246.
Royal Society manuscript PT. 17.2.
Read to the Royal Society 17 June.

R. *Ann. Phil.* ns 9 (1825):297–302.
The editor appended (pp. 301–302) a letter to Dr. T. S. Traill from Mr. Charles Horsefall, who had had his brig, *Tickler,* protected according to Davy's suggestions.
Phil. Mag. 65 (1825):203–206.
A. *Phil. Mag.* 64:233–234.
Quart. J. Sci. 17:279–280.
C. *Bibl. univ.* 29 (1825):31–39, 270–277; 30 (1825):526–527.
Ann. chim. 29 (1825):187–192.
Ann. Physik Chem. 3 (1825):211–220.

4.⋆ [Speech in eulogy of Mr. James Watt]

Works, VII, 140–145.
Davy's speech was delivered on 18 June, at the Freemasons' Hall in London.

5. Sir H. Davy and copper bottoms

The Times (London), 18 October.
Davy's letter of 17 October addressed to the editor defended his method for protecting copper sheeting on ships, and also defended his reputation against charges that he had had an ocean cruise at public expense.

6.⋆ [The presidential anniversary discourse—IV]

See 1827:1.
Read to the Royal Society on 30 November.

A. *Lit. Gaz.* p. 778.
Phil. Mag. 64:459–462.
Quart. J. Sci. 18:327–331.
Ann. Phil. ns 9 (1825):61–66.

1825

1.   Prospectus of a society for introducing and domesticating
     new breeds or varieties of animals, such as quadrupeds,
     birds, or fishes, likely to be useful in common life; and for
     forming a general collection in zoology

A.   *Phil. Mag.* 66:66–68.
        Drafted with Sir Thomas Stamford Raffles on 1 March.
        The subsequent prospectus was the work of Raffles,
        alone. (See introduction, p. 11.)

2.   [Letter to John Frederick Daniell]

     Quart. J. Sci. 20:79.
        Davy's letter, dated 5 June, was included in Daniell's
        paper (pp. 78–93) which queried the validity of the meteor-
        ological data published in *Phil. Trans.*

3.★ Further researches on the preservation of metals by electro-
     chemical means

     Phil. Trans. [115]:328–346.
     Read to the Royal Society 9 June.

R.   *Phil. Mag.* 67 (1826):89–100.
        Ann. Phil. ns 11 (1826):248–259.
A.   *Quart. J. Sci.* 19:271–273; 20 (1826):343–348.
        Ann. Phil. ns 10:66–67.
T.   *Jahrb. Chem. Physik* 56 (1829):434–456.
        Translated by Professor Marx of Braunschweig. A glowing
        tribute to Davy as a chemist able to apply his science to
        practical ends was supplied by the editor in a note.
C.   *Bibl. univ.* 29 (1825):270–277.
        Ann. Physik. Chem. 4:466–469.

4.★ [The presidential anniversary discourse—V]

        See 1827:1.
        Read to the Royal Society 30 November.

A.   *Phil. Mag.* 66:461.
        Quart. J. Sci. 20 (1826):304–306.
        Ann. Phil. ns 11 (1826):55–61.

1826

1.★ The Bakerian lecture. On the relations of electrical and chemical changes

> Phil. Trans. [116]:383–422.
> Royal Society manuscript PT. 18.18.
> > Davy's last Bakerian lecture, read to the Royal Society 8 June.

R. Phil. Mag. ns 1 (1827):31–38, 94–104, 190–199.
A. Ann. Phil. ns 12:62–65.
> Quart. J. Sci. 22:334–336.
T. Ann. chim. 33:276–322.
> > Translated by Anatole Riffault.
C. Giorn. fis. chim. storia nat. 9:462–467.
> Jahrb. Chem. Physik 52 (1828):33–74.
> > Extracted by Schweigger, who added long comments.
> Bibl. univ. 33:132–138.
> Z. Physik Math. (Wien) 2 (1827):447–461.
> Neues J. Pharm. Aerzte Apoth. Chem. 15:84–143.
> > Abstract based on Ann. chim., above. (Not seen.)

2.★ [The presidential Anniversary discourse—VI]

> See 1827:1.
> Read to the Royal Society 30 November.

A. Quart. J. Sci. 22:316–323.
> Phil. Mag. ns 1 (1827):60–65.

1827

1.★ Six discourses delivered before the Royal Society at their anniversary meetings, on the award of the Royal and Copley medals; preceded by an address to the society on the progress and prospects of science

> London: John Murray. 3 pp., l., [ix]–xi, 148. 28 cm. (Half-title: Humphry Davy's discourses, 1820–1826.)
> > Charles Babbage in his Passages from the life of a philosopher (London, 1864, pp. 187–189) charged Davy with extracting funds from the Royal Society to line his own pocket, by shrewd manipulation on the publication of this book. Babbage's charges were answered by John Davy, in 1864,

in a letter addressed to the editors of *Phil. Mag.*—28
(1864):480–484. Dr. Davy said that Davy received 500
guineas for the copyright of the work from Murray, and
that only 850 copies were printed. The questionable
financial arrangement was the purchase of 500 copies by
the Royal Society at the trade price of 15s. 3d.; Murray
realized £381 5s. from the transaction, a sum obviously
short of what he had paid Davy. *Phil. Trans.* for 1827 at
the Royal Society Library has been bound with the *Discourses*; a half dozen or so other copies that I have seen
in scattered libraries do not have the *Discourses* so bound.

A. *Edin. Rev.* 46 (1827):352–367.
    Reviewed by Henry Brougham.
    See 1820:3, 1821:8, 1822:2, 1823:7, 1824:6, 1825:4, 1826:2.

1828

1.⋆ On the phaenomena of volcanoes

Phil. Trans. [118]:241–250.
Read to the Royal Society 20 March.

R. *Phil. Mag.* ns 4:85–94.
A. *Edin. Phil. J.* 196–198.
    Phil. Mag. ns 3:373–374.
T. *Bibl. univ.* 39:21–38.
    Ann. chim., s. 2, 38:133–150.

2.⋆ An account of some experiments on the torpedo

Phil. Trans. [119]:15–18.
Read to the Royal Society 20 November.

R. *Phil. Mag.* 6 (1829):81–84.
A. *Phil. Mag.* 5 (1829):300.
T. *Ann. chim.*, s. 2, 41 (1829):438–443.
    Bibl. univ. 41:99–105.
    Jahrb. Chem. Physik 57 (1829):17–23.
       Translated from the Swiss version, above, partly as a
       memorial to Davy, but chiefly because the editor deemed
       the paper important.
    Ann. Physik Chem. 16 (1829):311–316.
C. *Jahrb. Chem. Physik.* 55 (1829):454–455.
       Translated from the abstract in *Phil. Mag.*, above.
    Ann. Physik Chem. 15 (1829):318.

{3.*} [Plan to improve the British Museum]

> *Works*, VII, 361–365.
>> John Davy extracted a section from an unpublished manuscript.

R. J. Z. Fullmer, *Chymia* 12 (1967):127–150.
> The full text of Davy's recommendations.

4. Salmonia: or days of fly fishing. In a series of conversations. With some account of the habits of fishes belonging to the genus salmo. By an angler [with plates]

> John Murray: London. viii, 273. 8°. BM. (Not seen.)

R. Another edition. 12°. Edinburgh. (Not seen.)
> The book was published in September, at an announced price of 10s. 6d.

A. *Lit. Gaz.* pp. 433–434; 451–454.
> Two reviews by different authors.
> *Blackwood's Magazine* 24:248–272.
> Reviewed by John Wilson.
> *Mirror* 12:253–254.
> The generation of eels.
> *Quart. Rev.* 38:503–535.
> Reviewed by Sir Walter Scott at Lady Davy's request.

C. *Bibl. univ.* 40 (1829):114–118.

1829

1.* Salmonia: or days of fly fishing. In a series of conversations. With some account of the habits of fishes belonging to the genus salmo. By an angler. [with plates.] London: John Murray. xiii, 335 pp. 8°
> The second edition, cited in BM (not seen).

R. The first American from the second London edition. Philadelphia: Carey and Lea, 1832. xii [13], 312 pp., 3 pl. 17.5 cm.
> Third edition [with plates]. London: John Murray. 1832. 3 l., [v]–xi, 1 l., 335 pp., 1 l. 17 cm.
> Fourth edition, with illustrations. London: John Murray, 1851. xvi, 1 l., 305 pp. 17 cm.
>> Edited by John Davy.
> An American edition, from the fourth London edition.

Boston: Roberts Brothers, 1870. xvi, 305 pp., illus. 17 cm.
Fifth edition. London: John Murray, 1869. 8°
   Cited in LC (not seen).
Another edition. London: John Murray, 1870. 12°
   Cited in ECB (not seen).

T. *Salmonia oder neun Angeltage. Unterhalten über Fische aus den Salmengeschlecht.* Deutsch bearbeitet von Carl Neubert. Mit 3 Abl. Leipzig, 1840. 8°.
   Cited in Heinsius (not seen).

1830

1.★ Consolations in travel, or the last days of a philosopher. Edited by John Davy.

London: John Murray. 1 p., l., [v]–vi, 3 l. 281, [1] pp. 17 cm. Published posthumously. The reprinting in *Collected Works* (vol. 7, pp. 207–388) contains part of an additional dialogue, VII, "On the chemical elements" (pp. 383–388) which John Davy did not include in the first edition. He took the fragment from another set of dialogues left in Davy's notebooks and changed the names of the discussants to make them uniform with those in *Consolations.* He did not include the two final paragraphs of the extant manuscript (see p. 14). The unprinted portion shows to what extent Sir Humphry had parted from the Boscovich atom, to which he alluded in the final, printed section (p. 388).

R. Consolations in travel, or the last days of a philosopher. By Sir Humphry Davy, Bart. Late President of the Royal Society. With a sketch of the author's life, and notes, by Jacob Green, M.D., Professor of Chemistry in Jefferson Medical College.
Philadelphia: John Grigg. Clark and Raser, Printer. 1830. 2 p., l., [iii]–iv, [5]–252. 15 × 9 cm.
The third edition. London: John Murray, 1831. vi, 264 pp. 8°
   Cited in BM (not seen).
The fourth edition. London: John Murray, 1838. vi, 264 pp. 8°
   Cited in BM (not seen).
The fifth edition, with illustrations. London: John Murray, 1851. iv, 297 pp.
   Cited in BM (not seen).

The sixth edition, with illustrations. London: John Murray, 1853. iv, 297 pp., illus. 18 cm.
>Edited by John Davy.

The seventh edition. London: John Murray, 1869. 12mo.
>Cited in ECB (not seen).

Another edition. Boston: Roberts Brothers, 1870. 2 pp., 1., [iii]–iv, 3 l., [3]–297 pp., front., illus. 17 cm.
>Edited by John Davy.

Another edition, without illustrations. London: Cassell, 1889. [Cassell's National Library, no. 203]. 192 pp. 16°
>Cited in BM (not seen).

A. *Edin. Phil. J.* pp. 320–325.
>An extract entitled "On the formation of the earth."

T. *Ultimos dias de un filosofo: conferencias sobre la naturaleza, las ciencias . . . con un prólogo . . . e interesantes notas por Camilo Flammarion.* Traduccion española de D. Abraham H. Inglesias y Coba y O. S. Comuñez Echeverria. Madrid, 1878. 332 pp. 8°
>Cited in *Edinburgh* and HSA (not seen).

Sir Humphry Davy's Tröstende Betrachtungen auf Reisen; oder die letzten Tage eines Naturforschers. Nach den 3ten Ausg. Verdeutscht von Carl Fr. Ph. von Martius. Nürnberg: Schrag, 1833 (1832). x, 305 pp. 8°
>Cited in BM (not seen).

Another edition. Nach d. 3 Ausg. verdeutscht v. C. Fr. Ph. v. Martius. 2 verb. Ausg. mit d. Bildnisse des Verfassers. Nürnberg: Schrag, 1839. 8°
>Cited in Heinsius (not seen).

Les derniers jours d'un philosophe. Entretiens sur la nature, les sciences, les métamorphoses de la terre et du ciel, l'humanité, l'âme, et la vie éternelle. Ouvrage traduit de l'anglais, accompagné d'une préface et de notes par Camille Flammarion. Paris: Didier, 1869. xxxii, 368 pp.
>Cited in BN (not seen).

Third edition. Paris: Didier, 1872. xxxii, 368 pp.
>Cited in BN (not seen).

Ninth edition. Paris: Didier, 1883. xxxii, 370 pp.
>Cited in BN (not seen).

En naturforskares sista dagar. Tysk öfvers. fran 3 engelska upplagan. Utgifven på svenska af Clemens Ullgren. Stockholm: Haeggström, 1834.
>Cited in SB (not seen).

Los ultimos dias de un filosofo. Dialogo sobre la naturaleza, las ciencias, las metamorfosis de la tierra y del cielo, la humanidad, el alma y la vida eterna. Traduccion del ingles por F. Luis Obiols. Barcelona: Talleres o Editorial Maneci, 1925. 298 pp. 19 × 12 cm.

Cited in *Española*, II, 14 (not seen).

1840

{1.⋆} [On Newton]

Works, VII, 124–127.

{2.⋆} [Electrical powers and irritability]

Works, VII, 352.

{3.⋆} [Extract from a geological lecture]

Works, VII, 353.

{4.⋆} [History of the natural sciences]

Works, VII, 321–323.

Index